Key skills for **kids**

DYSLEXIA

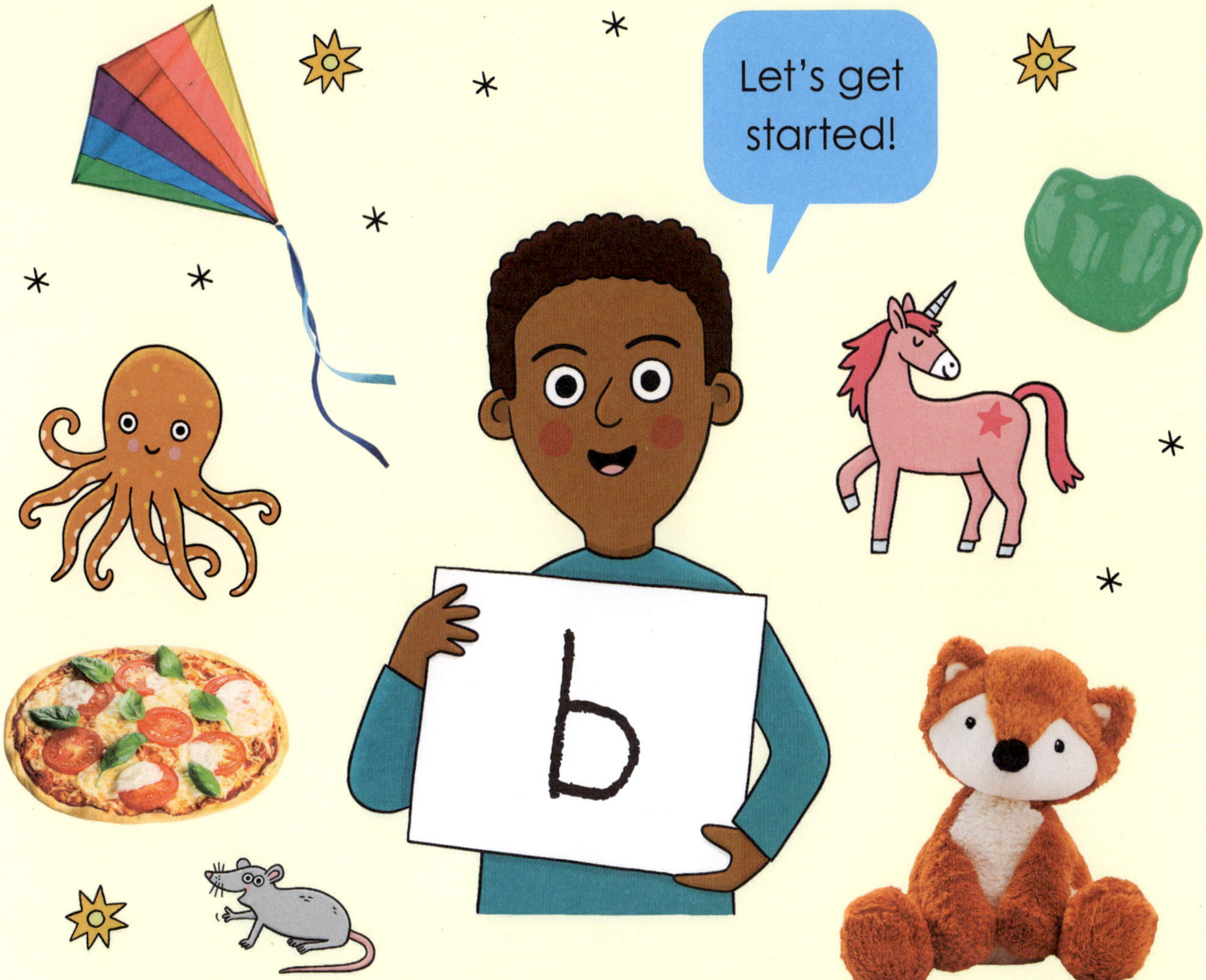
Let's get started!
b

priddy books
big ideas for little people

What is dyslexia?

Dyslexia is a specific **learning difficulty**. It affects how the brain handles information it **sees and hears**. Although everyone with dyslexia is different, your child may show the following:

- A poor quality of **written work** compared with oral ability
- Become **confused** by letters that look similar
- Have weak **reading fluency**
- Find it difficult to **blend letters** together
- Have an unusual **pronunciation** of words
- Poor reading **comprehension**
- A slow **processing speed** such as spoken and/or written language
- Poor **concentration**
- Difficulty following **instructions**
- Become **easily distracted**
- Have **memory difficulties** e.g., for daily routines and self-organization

Children with dyslexia may also have difficulty in these **three areas**:

- **Phonological awareness:** the ability to hear and distinguish between **sounds**
- **Verbal memory:** the ability to store and then recall **information** presented verbally
- **Verbal processing speed:** the fluency of the **verbal response** to information. For example, answering a question or carrying out an instruction

Aim of this book

Dyslexia is a lifelong learning difficulty. However we can **support** children with dyslexia by **developing different tools** that will help them with their **learning** and to become independent learners.

This book focuses on developing skills in two of the main areas of dyslexia: **phonological awareness** and **verbal memory**.

Each section **increases** in difficulty and provides plenty of opportunities for practice. The activities are designed to build up **both phonology and memory skills**, then reading, writing, and spelling ability.

Multisensory learning

This book also gives children a **multisensory learning experience**. This is the process of using **two or more senses** simultaneously while learning. By using more than one sense at once, **learning connections** are made even stronger.

We will highlight which **senses** are being used by the following **symbols**:

 Visual sense: The visual sense of **sight** is used when the child interprets things that they see, such as when reading text.

 Tactile sense: The tactile sense is used when the child **touches** the information to process it.

 Auditory sense: The auditory sense of **hearing** is used when the child hears the information that they are learning.

 Oral sense: The oral sense is used when the child uses **spoken language**.

Contents

How to use this book	6
Alphabet work	7
Parent tips	8
Tracking markers	10
Seek and find	11
Alphabet sequencing	12
Letter sounds	13
Alphabet tracking	14
All about vowels	15
Short vowels	16
Matching short vowels	17
Spell short vowel words	18
Write your own	19
Long vowel sound /a/	20
Long vowel sound /e/	21
Long vowel sound /i/	22
Long vowel sound /o/	23
Long vowel sound /u/	24
Short or long vowel /a/	25
Short or long vowel /e/	26
Short or long vowel /i/	27
Short or long vowel /o/	28
Short or long vowel /u/	29
Which short vowel sound?	30
Long vowel sounds	31
Macron and breve	32
Handwriting practice	33
Phonological awareness	35
Parent tips	36
Rhyme Time: Hey Diddle Diddle	38
Rhyme Time: Incy Wincy Spider	39
Rhyme Time: Humpty Dumpty	40
Rhyming pairs	41
Find the rhyme	42
Write the rhyme	43
Make a rhyme	44
Same sounds	45
Which vowel?	46
Where is the "ă" sound?	47
/s/ sound	48
End sounds	49
How many syllables?	50
Segmenting syllables	51
Blending syllables	52
Complete the word	53
Onset and rime	54
Blending	55
Segmenting	56
Phonemic awareness	57
Blending sounds	58
Memory	59
Parent tips	60
Repeat it!	62
Picture patterns	63
More patterns	64

Break it down!	65
Chunking	66
Picture it!	68
Picture this	69
Letter sequences	70
More sequences	71
Picture memory	73
Remember it!	74
Copy me	75
Memory dots	76
My house	77
Bouncy balls	78
Dino world	79
Which sentence?	81
Listen and color	82
Copy image	84
Tricky words	86
Sight words	88
Reading	89
Parent tips	90
High-frequency words	92
Flash cards	93
High-frequency word search	95
Create your own	96
Reading CVC words	97
Reading CCVC words	98
Reading CVCC words	99
Four in a row	100
Complete the sentence	101
More sentences	102
Understand the text	103
My alien	104
Summarizing	105
Time for school	106
Beach day	107
Happy birthday!	108
Writing	109
Parent tips	110
Spider diagram	112
My spider diagram	113
Writing sentences	114
Build on a sentence	115
Choose again	117
Free-write	118
Create your own	119
Answers	120
Glossary	126
Additional resources	127
Author biographies	127
Contributors & credits	128

Answers are on pages 120–125!

How to use this book

Although most activities are designed for children to work on **independently**, some children may **require support** to read the questions and text. It is useful to always be on hand to help your child with the activities. It would also be **advisable** to read the **parent guides** at the start of each section and the tips throughout. Any activities that need specific **adult help** will be highlighted with this symbol.

What order should my child do the activities in?

It is recommended to work through each section in the **order of pages** and the activities within each page. However, it is also a good idea to work on all five sections **simultaneously**. For example

- On **day one,** your child can focus on some alphabet exercises;
- On **day two,** your child can work on improving their phonological awareness;
- On **day three**, your child can focus on enhancing their verbal memory skills, and so on.

Use the **bookmarks** attached when you need to cover up part of an activity.

How frequently should my child do the activities?

Little and often is recommended.

How long should each activity take?

Each activity should take between **10 to 15 minutes**. This includes checking answers and making any necessary changes.

How can I help my child if they become frustrated or find an activity difficult?

If your child is finding a task difficult, you can work through the activity with them. Take **regular breaks** and always make sure to celebrate what they have done well in each activity.

ALPHABET WORK

Parent tips: Alphabet work

What is it?

It often takes children who have dyslexia longer to learn which letters **correspond** to which sounds.

The ability to **recall** this information straightaway is required for successful reading and writing.

Aim

These exercises will improve your child's **confidence** in recognizing letters and the sounds they make. They will also help to make your child a better reader, writer, and speller.

Letter names & sounds

It is important to introduce both **letter names** and **letter sounds** and distinguish between the two so that children recognize that letter names match with letter sounds.

Letter names are used when spelling. They are pronounced as: A: ay; B: bee; C: see, etc.

Letter sounds are used when reading and are pronounced quite differently from letter names. The chart on the inside back cover shows your child how to pronounce letter sounds. There are also lots of great learning resources online to help with this.

Tracking

There are **four letters** in the alphabet that are extra important:
the first letter of the alphabet **(a)**
the last letter of the alphabet **(z)**
the two middle letters of the alphabet **(m, n)**.

These are called the **four markers**. When working on alphabet sequencing, it is important that children can identify them.

Alphabet arc

At the back of the book, you will find a removable **alphabet arc**. This arc contains the 26 letters of the alphabet on one side.

The **alphabet arc** is designed to help your child identify the next letter in the alphabet sequence by locating the positioning of the markers. The four markers are highlighted in the color red.

Remove the arc and keep it visible throughout the **alphabet worksheets** in this section.

Skills

- **Sequencing** of the alphabet
- Matching letter sounds to letter names **(letter-sound correspondence)**

Tips

- Keep the **front side of the alphabet arc** in front of your child for each of the activities so that they can refer back to it. Any activities that the arc will be needed for will have the arc symbol.

- It is recommended that letter-sound correspondence is practiced for **5 to 10 minutes daily**.

- Once your child is confident, **challenge** your child to complete the activities without the arc. The arc can be used to check if the answers are correct.

9

Tracking markers

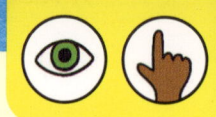

The four tracking markers are the first letter of the alphabet (a), the last letter of the alphabet (z), and the two middle letters of the alphabet (m, n).

1. Circle the four markers when you see them in each row. They may be in a different order.

ⓐ ⓜ w e l d o ⓝ r ⓩ q w o

x q u t y z n a m p w u e

o z c b n t y w e p l m a

z q y r e d a i p x f n m

a v t e w g l m n i o p z

 Keep your pencil on the page for each line as the example shows and use your alphabet arc to help.

Seek and find

1. Can you find each of the four markers in the scene?

2. Find the alphabet arc at the back of the book.
Can you trace over the four markers?
Say the letter names and letters sounds as you trace!

 If you are not sure what the letters or sounds are, ask an adult to help you.

Alphabet sequencing

1) Can you fill in the missing letters on each of the trains?

1. a b c _ _ f _ h _ j _ l

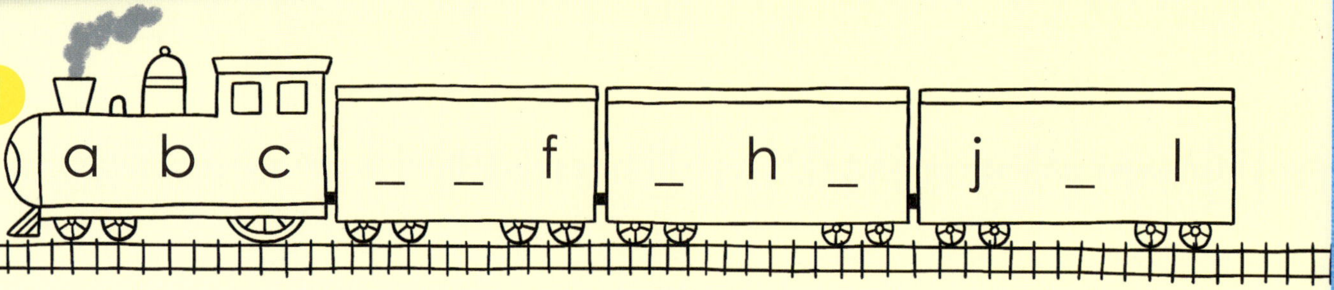

2. d e _ g h _ _ k _ m n _

3. p _ _ s t _ v _ _ y _

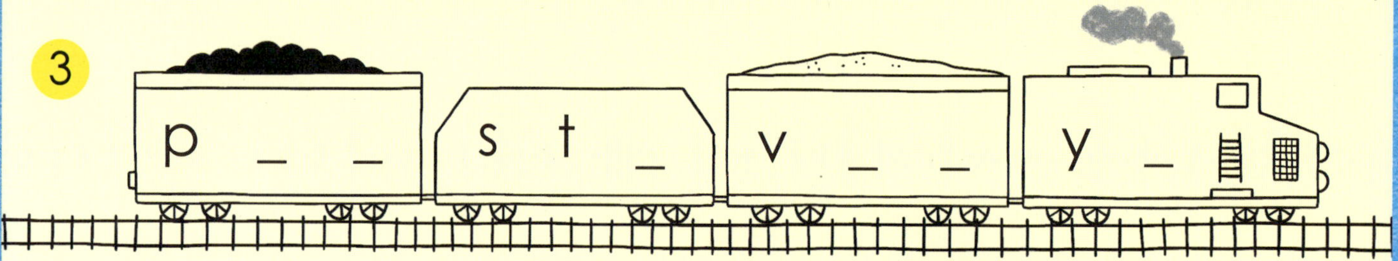

4. t _ v _ _ _ z

2) Now can you circle each of the four markers when you see them on the trains?

One of the markers appear more than once.

Letter sounds

We pronounce letter sounds in a different way from letter names.

1. Trace over the letters, saying their sounds at the same time. The chart on the inside back cover will help.

start here

a b c d e f g

h i j k l m n

o p q r s t u

v w x y z

Can you trace over each letter three times while saying the letter sound? This helps the shape of the letter and its sound stick in your memory.

Alphabet tracking

1. Can you fill in the whole lowercase alphabet?

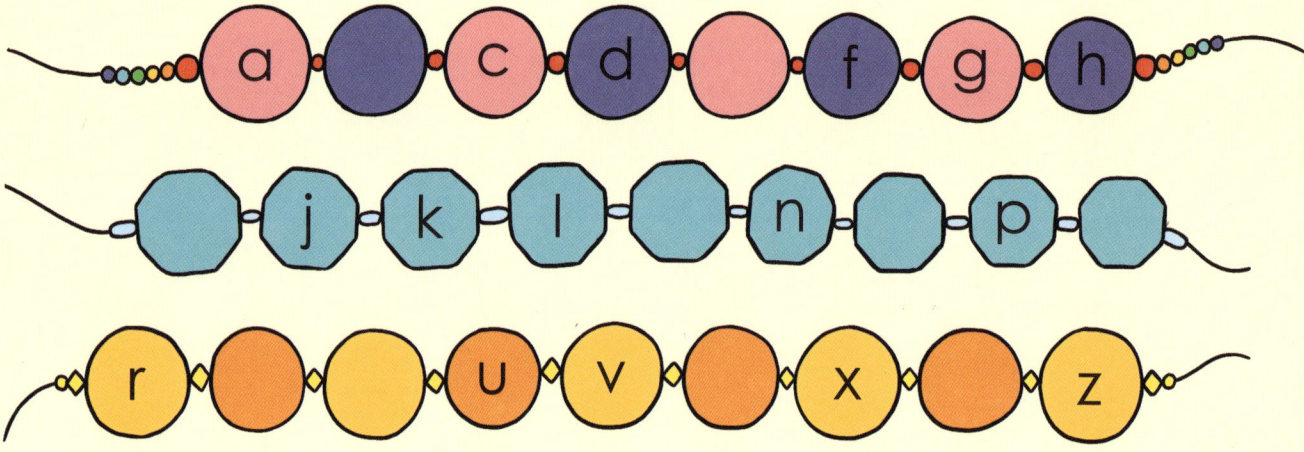

2. Can you fill in the whole uppercase alphabet?

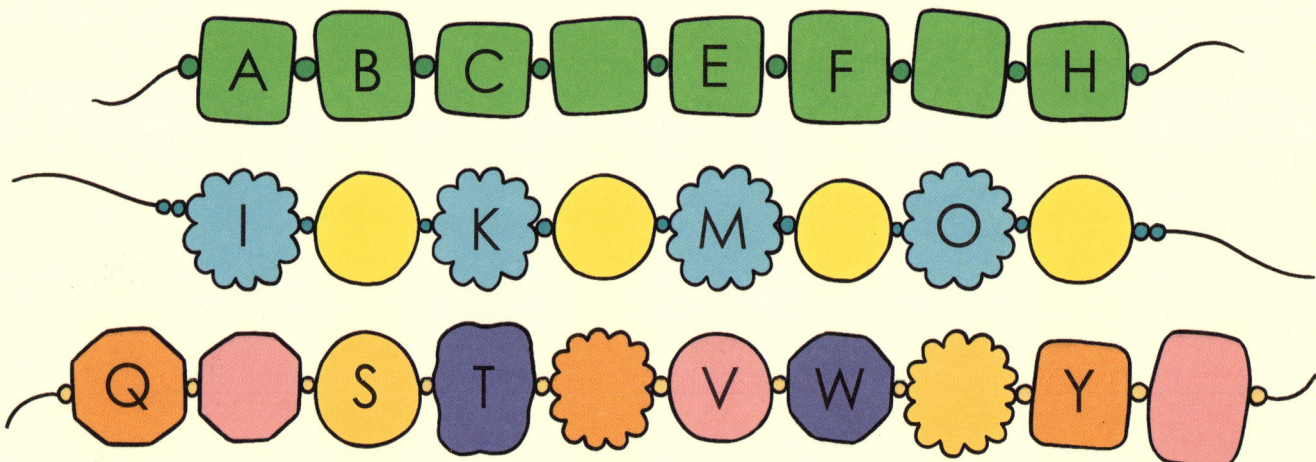

 Use your alphabet arc to help you to remember the sequence of the alphabet.

All about vowels

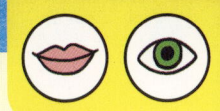

There are five vowels in the English language.

a e i o u

Vowel sounds are important, as they are found in every word. Help your child remember the vowels by using this sentence:

Athletic **E**lephants **I**n **O**ctopus **U**nderpants.

1. Can you try saying the different short vowel sounds and long vowel sounds?

Short vowel		Long vowel	
🍏	a as in apple	🦧	a as in ape
🥚	e as in egg	🐑	e as in sheep
🧊	i as in igloo	🍨	i as in ice cream
🐙	o as in octopus	🌾	o as in oats
🧶	u as in rug	🦄	u as in unicorn

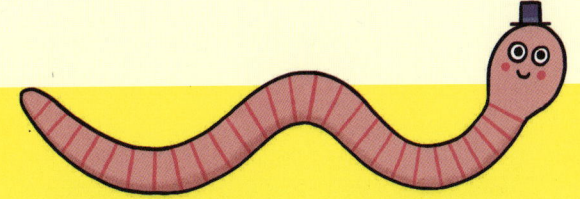

Our mouths stay open for longer when we say long vowel sounds.

Short vowels

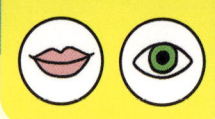

1. Draw a circle around the short vowel sound that matches each picture.

cap cep	
nat net	
pig pag	
box bax	
mug mig	

Sound out each word first to see which one matches the picture.

Matching short vowels

1 Draw a line from each word to its short vowel sound.

| a | e | i | o | u |

10
ten

flag

hat

bed

sun

fox

tin

egg

6
six

Say the words aloud to help you spot the correct sound.

Spell short vowel words

1. Fill in the gaps to spell the short vowel words.

_ u _   _ a _   _ i _   _ _ o _   _ e _

2. Fill in the gaps to spell the short vowel words.

_ _ _   _ _ _   _ _ _   _ _ _   _ _ _

Say the words aloud to help you to hear the sounds.

Write your own

1. Using the letters below, can you write the short vowel words that match the pictures?

a s b l g t u o b

....

....

....

Long vowel sound /a/

1 Circle all of the pictures that have a long vowel /a/ sound.

snake	pizza	pet	igloo

boat	lake	grape	rope

tail	green	paint	spoon

Look back at page 15 to help you remember the short and long vowel sounds.

Long vowel sound /e/

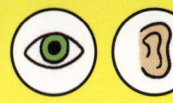

1 Circle all of the pictures that have a long vowel **/e/** sound.

sheep	rock	leaf	sleep

dog	ape	fox	pea
			3
hat	beach	bag	three

Remember to say the words aloud to hear the long vowel sound. Look back at page 15 for help.

Long vowel sound /i/

1 Circle all of the pictures that have a long vowel /i/ sound.

spices	mice	bowl	bike
	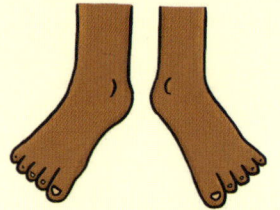		
kite	feet	rice	beans

train	time	hen	pie

Look back at page 15 to help you remember how to say the short and long vowel sounds.

Long vowel sound /o/

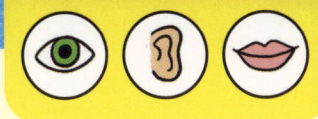

1 Circle all of the pictures that have a long vowel /o/ sound.

| rope | toast | milk | boat |

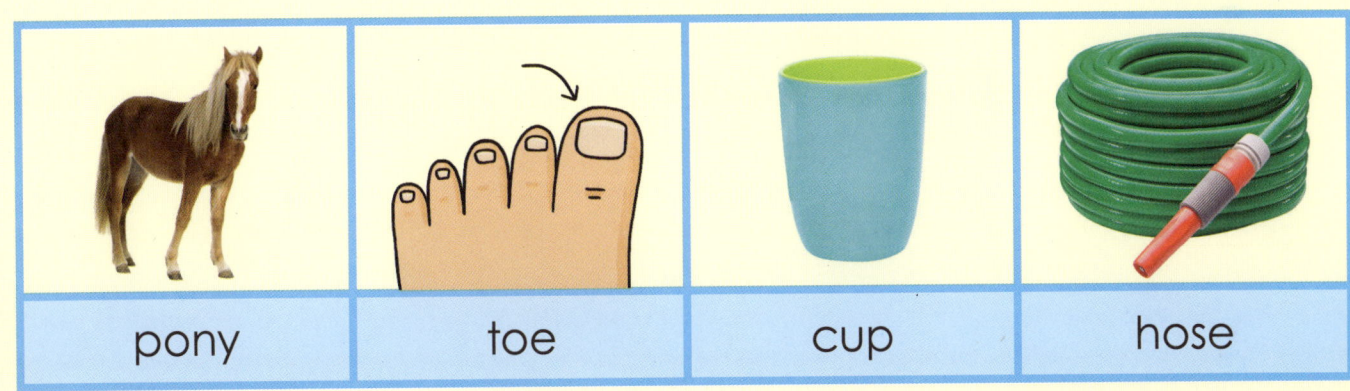

| pony | toe | cup | hose |

| stick | cone | sock | road |

Your mouth is open longer when you make a long vowel sound. Look back at page 15 to help you remember the sounds.

Long vowel sound /u/

1 Circle all of the pictures that have a long vowel /u/ sound.

music	nine	uniform	cube

flute	leaf	pupil	cute

		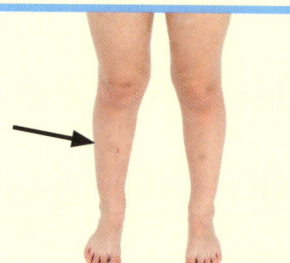	
huge	unicorn	mug	leg

Look back at page 15 to help you remember how to say the short and long vowel sounds.

Short or long vowel /a/

1 Do these words have a short vowel sound or a long vowel sound? Check the correct box.

	Short vowel /a/	Long vowel /a/
cake		
bag		
baby		
cat		
rain		

Look back at page 15 to help you remember the short and long vowel sounds.

Short or long vowel /e/

1 Do these words have a short vowel sound or a long vowel sound? Check the correct box.

	Short vowel /e/	Long vowel /e/
bell		
feet		
red		
leg		
sea		

Short or long vowel /i/

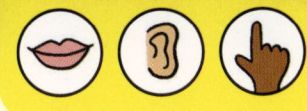

1 Do these words have a short vowel sound or a long vowel sound? Check the correct box.

	Short vowel /i/	Long vowel /i/
wig		
ice cream		
igloo		
kite		
fish		

Short or long vowel /o/

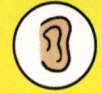

1 Do these words have a short vowel sound or a long vowel sound? Check the correct box.

	Short vowel /o/	Long vowel /o/
goat		
cog		
doll		
sock		
loaf		

Short or long vowel /u/

1. Do these words have a short vowel sound or a long vowel sound? Check the correct box.

	Short vowel /u/	Long vowel /u/
tube		
rug		
cube		
duck		
huge		

Say the words aloud to help with identifying the sound.

Which short vowel sound?

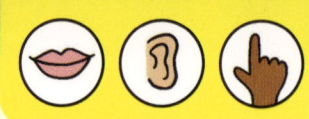

1 Look at each of the pictures below.
Which is the first short vowel sound that you hear?
Write the vowel in the space underneath.

man	egg	log
a		

fox	pig	sun

Remember that the five vowels are: a, e, i, o, and u.

Long vowel sounds

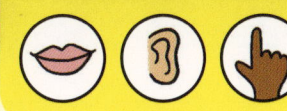

1. Look at each of the pictures below.
   Which is the first long vowel sound that you hear?
   Write the vowel in the space underneath.

ice cream	unicorn	sheep
i		

gate	bee	bone

Macron and breve

We can use symbols to show that a sound is long or short.

The macron is a symbol for a long vowel sound. ―

shēep

In the word "sheep", the **/e/** is a long vowel, so we would place a macron above it.

The breve is a symbol for a short vowel sound. ˘

căt

In the word "cat," the **/a/** is a short vowel, so we would place a breve above it.

1 Color in the words that need a macron orange and the words that need a breve purple.

bib	goat
hat	rug
fox	rain
sleep	pig

2 Once you have completed Activity 1, why not add a macron or breve symbol above each of the vowel sounds?

Handwriting practice

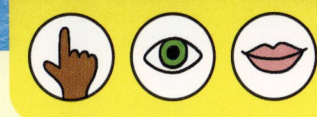

Practicing handwriting letters regularly helps to train your child's brain to remember the shapes of letters. This is a useful skill for spelling.

1 Can you practice writing each of the letters?

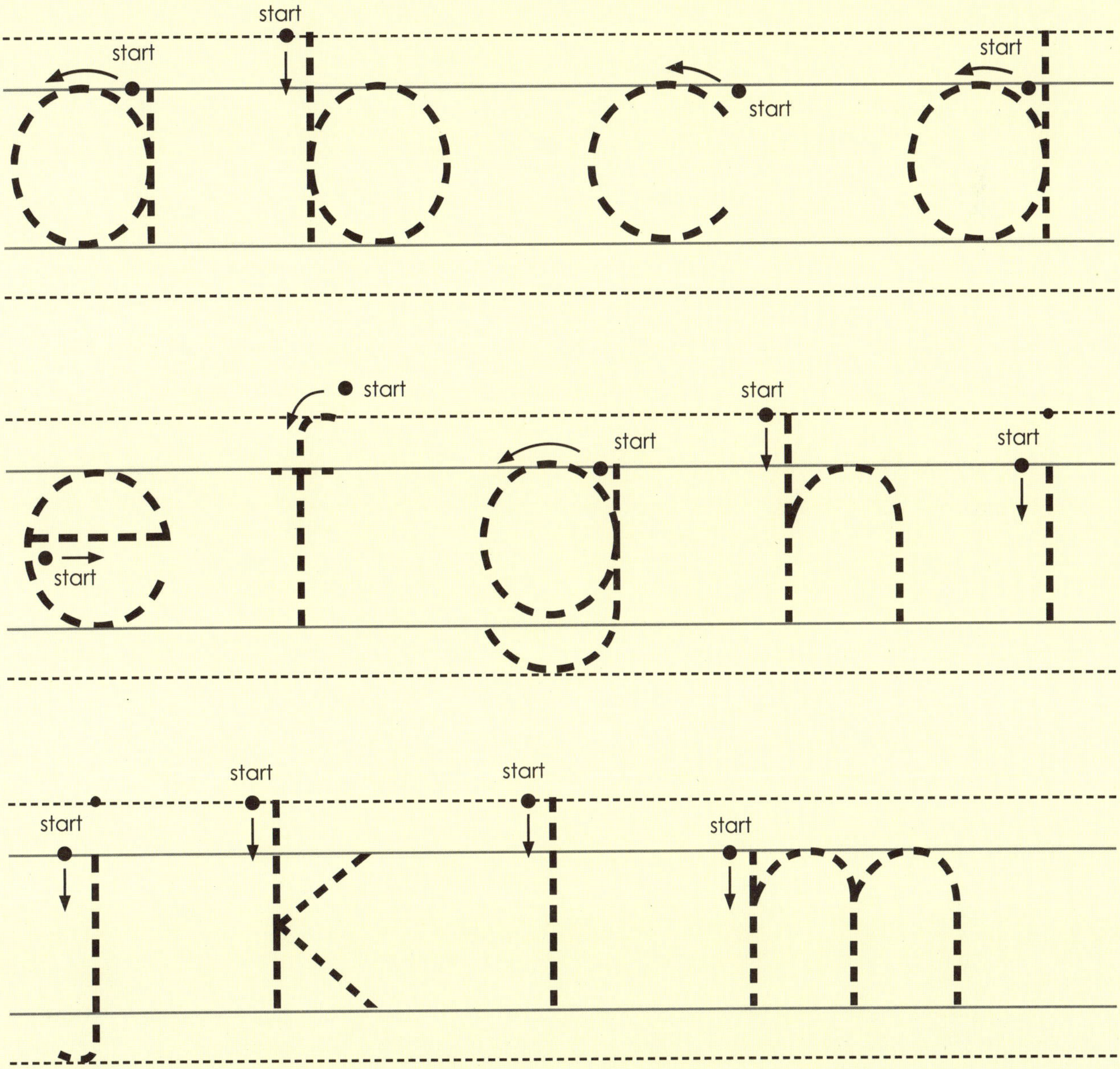

a b c d

e f g h i

j k l m

2 Can you practice writing each of the letters?

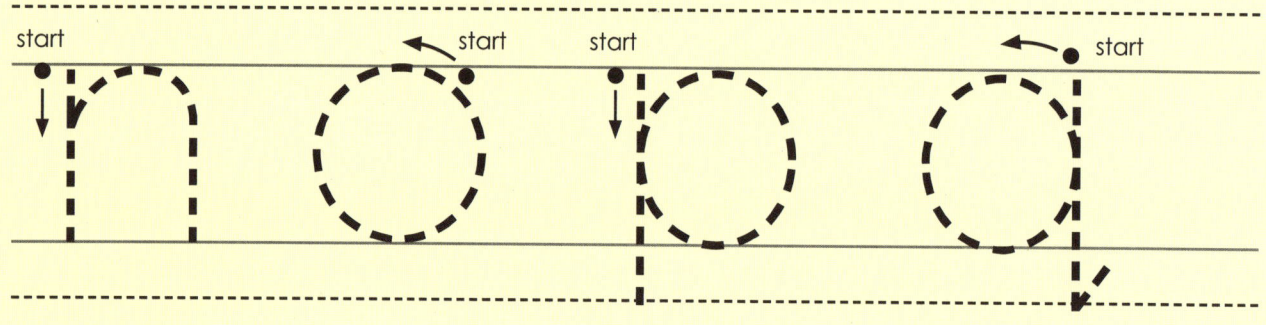

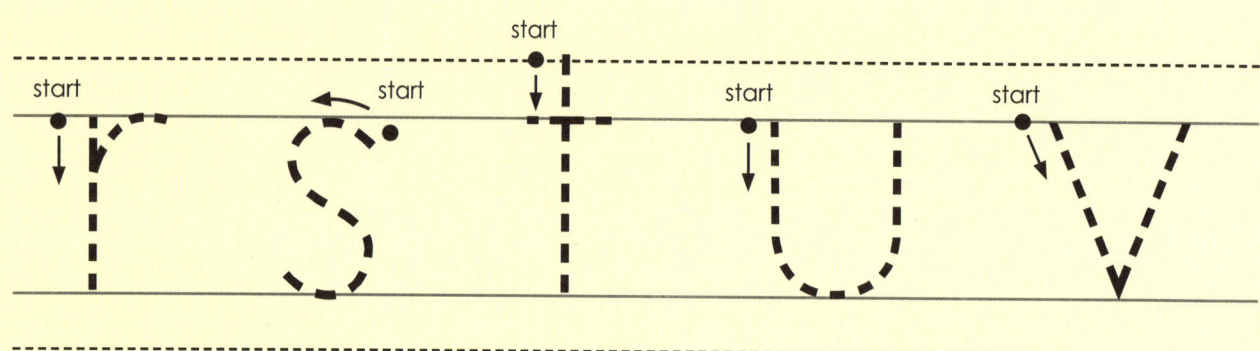

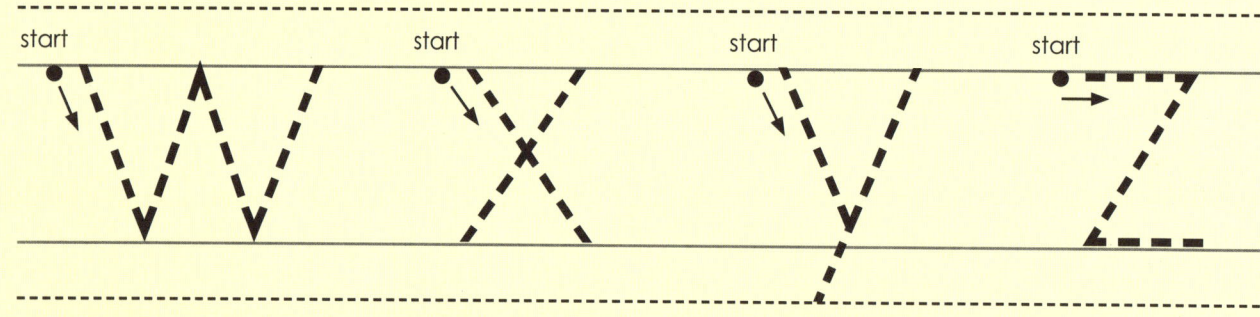

Make sure to follow the arrows to form the letters.

PHONOLOGICAL AWARENESS

Parent tips: Phonological awareness

What is it?

Phonological awareness is the understanding of the sound structure in words and the ability to hear and recognize them.

It involves the following skills:

- **identifying** sounds
- **discriminating** between sounds
- **taking apart** the sounds in words
- **blending** sounds together to make a word

These skills are crucial in helping children build an awareness of how letters and sounds go together in words (**sound structure**), making it easier to learn to read and write.

Aim

As children with dyslexia struggle to learn the sound structure of words, this can affect their ability to read, write, and spell.

In this section, children will start to build an **awareness** of how letters and sounds go together in words. This will help them to read and write more **efficiently** and gain more confidence.

There are **five stages** that we will look at in this section:

Skills

Stage 1. Rhyme awareness and construction:
The ability to hear **rhymes** within words, recognize rhyming words, and produce rhyming words.

Stage 2. Sound and word discrimination:
Your child can hear **units of sounds** within a sentence, and is able to identify which word is different. Children who have difficulty in this area may struggle to identify the differences between certain words, such as "hot" and "hit."

Stage 3: Syllabification:
When your child can break down words into individual **syllables** and then blend them together.

Stage 4: Onset and rime:
Teaching your child about word families. The **onset** is the part of a single-syllable word before the vowel. The **rime** is the part of a word including the vowel and the letters after it. In the word "pig:" "p" is the onset and "ig" would be the rime.

Stage 5: Phonemic awareness:
When your child can **blend sounds** into words, break up words into sounds, and delete or move around sounds in words.

Tips

- Try fun **rhyming games** that allow your child to recognize similar-sounding words.
- Encourage your child to **clap out** the syllables in words to help them break down words into small manageable parts.
- Practice **saying words** slowly and deliberately. This helps your child become more aware of individual sounds and how the sounds form words.

Rhyme time: Hey Diddle Diddle

Stage 1

1. Ask a grown-up to read the nursery rhyme.

Hey diddle diddle,
The cat and the fiddle,
The cow jumped over the moon;
The little dog laughed to see such fun,
And the dish ran away with the spoon.

2. Ask a grown-up to repeat the nursery rhyme. Why not join in?

3. Can you underline all the words that rhyme in the nursery rhyme above?

Rhyming words are words that end with the same sound. For example, the words "cat" and "hat" rhyme, as they both end in the /at/ sound.

Rhyme time: Itsy Bitsy Spider

Stage 1

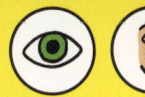

1. Ask a grown-up to read the nursery rhyme.

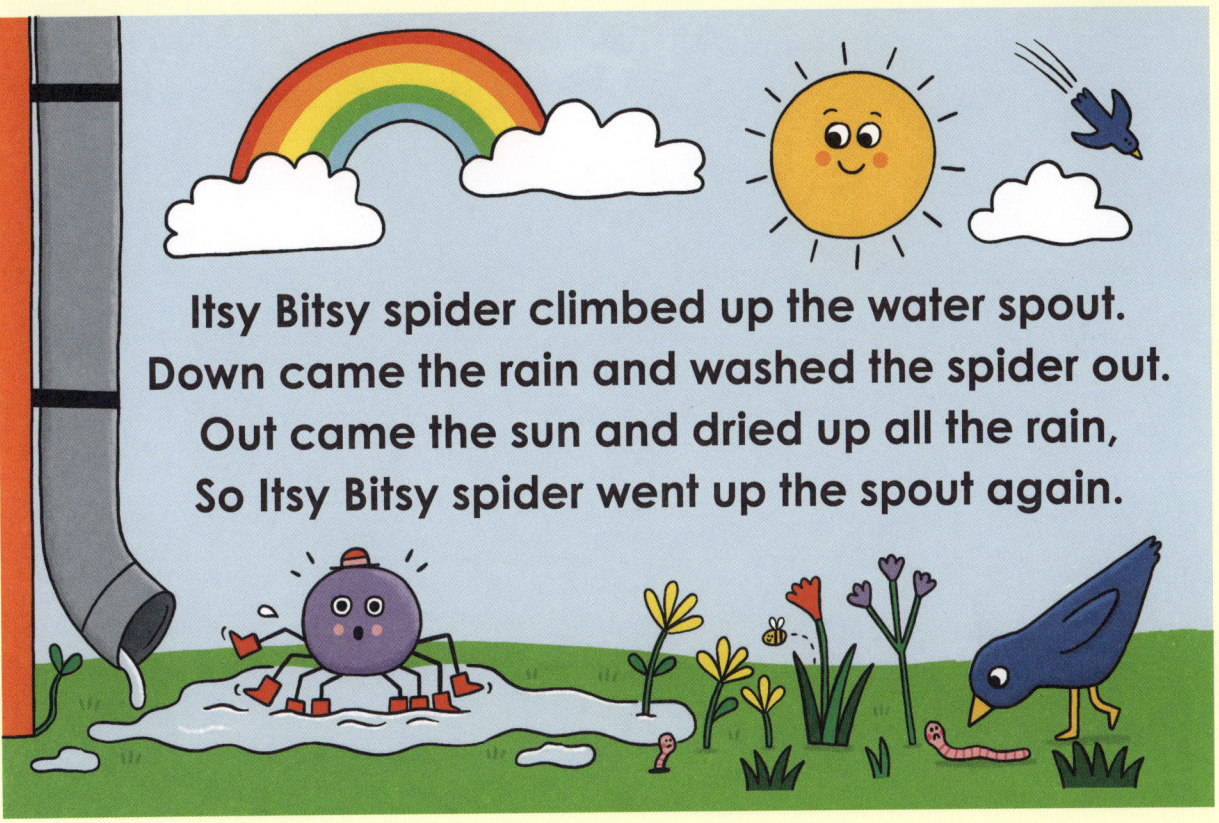

Itsy Bitsy spider climbed up the water spout.
Down came the rain and washed the spider out.
Out came the sun and dried up all the rain,
So Itsy Bitsy spider went up the spout again.

2. Ask a grown-up to repeat the nursery rhyme. Why not join in?

3. Can you underline the words that rhyme in the nursery rhyme above?

Rhyme time: Humpty Dumpty

Stage 1

1. Ask a grown-up to read the nursery rhyme.

Humpty Dumpty sat on a wall.
Humpty Dumpty had a great fall.
All the king's horses and all the king's men,
Couldn't put Humpty together again.

2. Ask a grown-up to repeat the nursery rhyme. Why not join in?

3. Can you underline the words that rhyme in the nursery rhyme above?

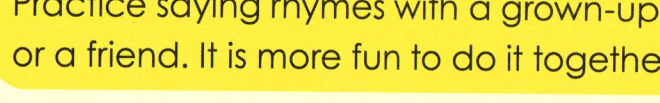

Practice saying rhymes with a grown-up or a friend. It is more fun to do it together!

Stage 2

Rhyming pairs

1 Circle the word in each row that rhymes with the first picture.

map	cap	ten	jug

skip	vet	hip	pot

fun	stop	sun	log

Remember, only one word in each row rhymes.

Find the rhyme

Stage 2

1 Look at the pictures below.
Circle all the words that rhyme with "cat."

hat

net

rat

mug

fox

hit

grin

bat

Rhyming words are words that end with the same sound.

42

Write the rhyme

Stage 2

1. Choose the correct rhyming words for each picture. Write them in the table below.

Rhyming words		
fog	bog	hog
chin	thin	spin
grin	log	tin

dog	pin

Remember, rhyming words are words that end with the same sound.

Make a rhyme

Stage 2

1 Finish the sentences by adding in a word that rhymes with the underlined words.

| sat | frog | see |

The cat went and _ _ _ on the bed.

The bee can _ _ _ the hive.

The dog made friends with the _ _ _ _.

Same sounds

Stage 2

Children need to be able to identify the differences and similarities between sounds. Sounds are also known as "phonemes."

1 Can you underline the letter in each pair of words that has the same sound?

| nut ran | bat cob |

| tag pet | hop hut |

Say the words aloud to help you hear the similar sounds.

45

Which vowel?

Stage 2

1 Fill in the missing vowel in each pair of words so that they have the same vowel sound.

	top	h _ t
	bed	m _ t
	cup	r _ b
	fin	f _ t
	sad	f _ n

Remember that the five vowels are a, e, i, o, and u.

Where is the "ă" sound?

Stage 2

1 Where can you hear the /ă/ sound in each word? Check the correct box under each picture.

m a t

a d d

b a g

d a d

c a t

a c t

When you say the word "pat" aloud, the first sound that you hear is /p/, the second sound is /ă/, and the last sound is /t/.

/s/ sound

Stage 2

1 Where can you hear the **/s/** sound in each word? Check the correct box under each picture.

s u m   s a d   s i t
□ □ □   □ □ □   □ □ □

s o n   b u s   s i x
□ □ □   □ □ □   □ □ □

y e s   a s k   s i p
□ □ □   □ □ □   □ □ □

Remember to say the words aloud so you can hear the sounds.

End sounds

Stage 2

1. Check the words in each row which have the same end sound as the first word.

stop	cap ○	pet ○	mop ○

can	pen ○	pin ○	bag ○

jet	bat ○	leg ○	hut ○

Say the words aloud to hear the end sound.

How many syllables?

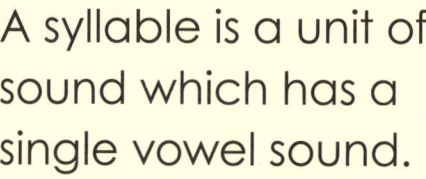
Stage 3

A syllable is a unit of sound which has a single vowel sound.

The word "cat" has one syllable. How many beats do you hear? 1!
The word "hero" has two syllables. How many beats do you hear? 2!
The word "basketball" has three syllables. How many beats do you hear? 3!

1 Circle the number of syllables in each of these words.

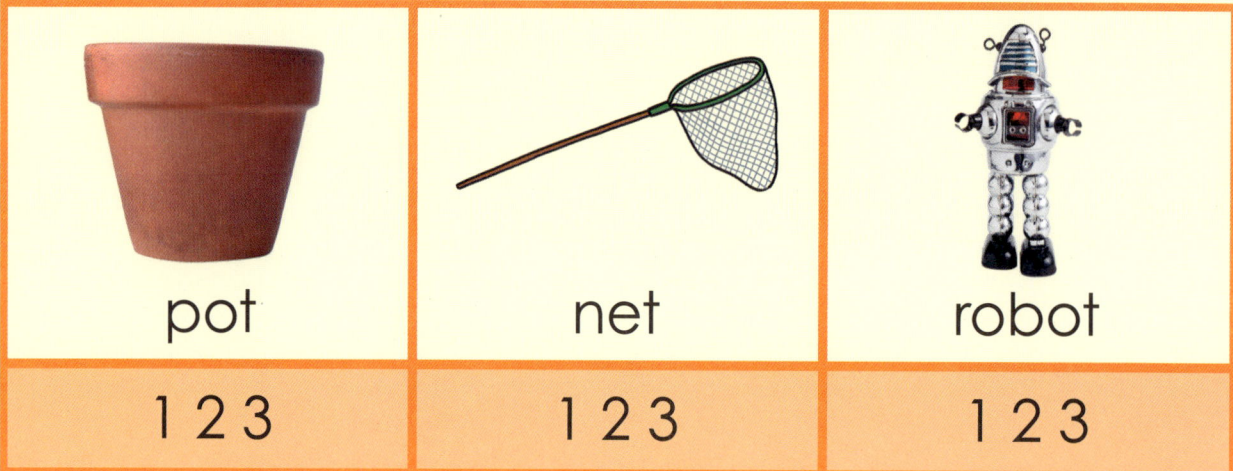

pot	net	robot
1 2 3	1 2 3	1 2 3

lemon	computer	sock
1 2 3	1 2 3	1 2 3

You can clap to help count the beats in a word.
In the word "bingo," the syllables are "bin" and "go."
Clap when you say "bin" and again for "go."

Stage 3

Segmenting syllables

Syllable segmentation is to take a word and break it down into its individual syllables.

For example, the word "chimpanzee" has three syllables: chim / pan / zee.

1 Can you break these words down into their individual syllables?

	carrot	_ _ _ / _ _ _
	tiger	_ _ / _ _ _
	dinosaur	_ _ / _ _ / _ _ _ _
	helicopter	_ _ _ / _ / _ _ _ / _ _ _

51

Blending syllables

Stage 3

Syllable blending is blending individual syllables back together to form a word.

For example, if you blend the two syllables "ta / ble" together, they become the word "table."

1. Following the example above, can you blend these syllables together to form each word?

🐰	rab/bit	_ _ _ _ _ _
💻	com/pu/ter	_ _ _ _ _ _ _ _
🦜	par/rot	_ _ _ _ _ _
🐛	cat/er/pil/lar	_ _ _ _ _ _ _ _ _ _ _

Complete the word

Stage 3

1. Draw a line to match up the two syllables to make the correct word.

trum	ten
ten	fin
muf	nis
kit	pet

53

Onset and rime

Stage 4

Onset is the initial sound in a word.
Rime is the letters that follow.

For example, in the word "fox," "**f**" is the onset and "**ox**" is the rime.
Not all words have onsets, such as the word "ax" which starts with a vowel.

1 Can you split each word into the onset and rime? The first one has been done for you.

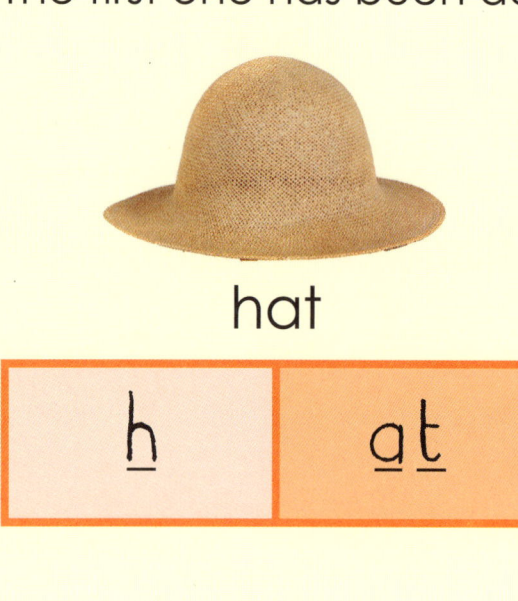

hat

| h | at |

red

| _ | _ _ |

mug

| _ | _ _ |

sit

| _ | _ _ |

Blending

Stage 4

1. Can you add the first sound to finish each of the words?

🚌	_ us
🗺️	_ ap
🐶	_ og
🐔	_ en

Segmenting

Stage 4

1. Following the example, remove the first sound from each word.

hot	h	o t
bat	_	_ _
leg	_	_ _
win	_	_ _

Read the words slowly to help you hear the first sound.

Phonemic awareness

Stage 5

Phonemic awareness is blending, segmenting, deleting, and moving sounds in words.

1 Can you break down these words into their individual sounds?

sad

wag

/s/ /a/ /d/   /_/ /_/ /_/

fog

top

/_/ /_/ /_/   /_/ /_/ /_/

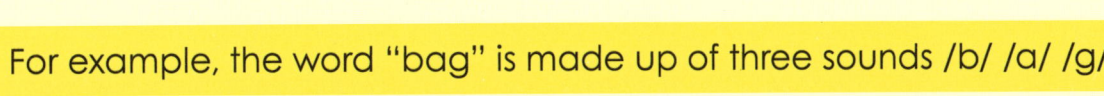
For example, the word "bag" is made up of three sounds /b/ /a/ /g/.

Blending sounds

Stage 5

1 Can you blend these sounds together to make each word?

/r/ /o/ /ck/
_ _ _ _

/d/ /i/ /g/
_ _ _

/r/ /a/ /t/
_ _ _

/sl/ /u/ /g/
_ _ _ _

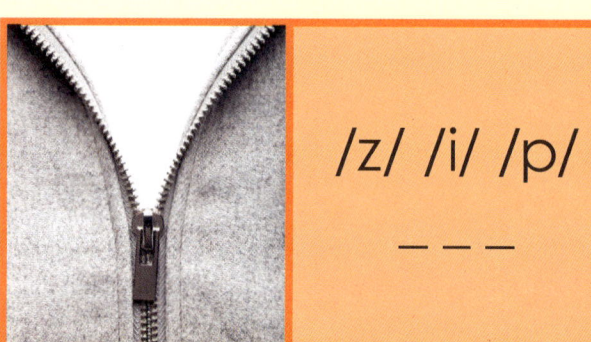

/z/ /i/ /p/
_ _ _

/d/ /u/ /ck/
_ _ _ _

MEMORY

Parent tips: Memory

What is it?

Memory can be divided into two types: **short-term memory** and **working memory**.

- **Short-term memory** is when we remember something for a short time and use it right away.
- **Working memory** is when we remember something, change it, and then respond to it.

Memory can also be broken down into two smaller areas called **visual** and **verbal memory**.

- **Visual memory** is our ability to remember what we see. For example, remembering sight words in reading or remembering sequences of movement in a dance.
- **Verbal memory** is our ability to use and remember what we hear. For example, following instructions or remembering key vocabulary that is introduced.

It is important to understand that children with dyslexia have difficulties with **memory**, such as forgetting conversations, tasks they have promised to do, or important dates.

Children may find it difficult to **recall** the names of people they have met. Dyslexia can also impact their ability to remember information they have learned in school.

It can be frustrating for children, but with patience and understanding, you can work together to **develop strategies** to cope with these challenges and help children to succeed.

Aim

The main aim of **memory training** is to improve your child's ability to remember and recall information. This will make it easier for children to **remember** taught methods and procedures which will help them to become better at working independently.

Skills

It is important that we support children with dyslexia by **teaching** them tools that they can use at school to help with their learning. There are many different **memory tools** that can be used and your child may even develop their own.

In this section, your child will learn **three tools** that are commonly used to help with memory training.

These three tools are:

- **Repetition:** repeating information over and over again
- **Chunking:** breaking down information into smaller groups to make it easier to remember
- **Visualization:** visualizing the information so that when it is removed, you can still picture what it is

Tips

- **Remind** your child to use these tools in their wider learning. This will help the memory tools become an **automatic skill**.

- **Make learning multisensory**: try to use as many senses as possible at the same time. For example, when reading information, say it aloud at the same time. Or when remembering sequences, picture them in your head while repeating them. This is something called "**dual coding**" and it helps children make stronger memory connections.

Use the removable **bookmarks** to cover up activities when needed.

Repeat it!

Mind tool

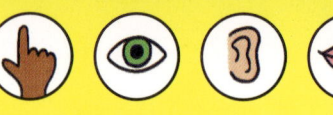

The first memory tool we are going to use is called **repetition**.

Repetition is when we repeat information several times so that it moves into our long-term memory.

1 Look at each shape below. Touch each shape with your finger and say its name at the same time.

triangle   triangle   circle

2 Now say the name of each shape again: triangle, triangle, circle. Repeat this three times.

Close your eyes and say the names of the shapes aloud. Did you get them right?

Picture patterns

1.

   cow   cow   sheep   horse

   Look at the pictures above, then cover them up. Can you use the repetition tool to remember what they were? Write their names or draw them below.

2.

   pig   pig   sheep   cow

   Look at the pictures above, then cover them up. Can you use the repetition tool to remember what they were? Write their names or draw them below.

Remember, use your bookmark to cover up the pictures!

More patterns

1.

   clock   house   chair   cup   table

   Look at the pictures above. Now cover them up.

2. Keeping the images above covered, look at the pictures below. Which one is missing? Write or draw it in the space.

   clock   house   cup   table

Remember to use the repetition tool to remember the images.

Break it down!

Mind tool

Our next memory tool is **chunking**. This is when we break down information into small, manageable chunks.

Look at the images above. That's a lot to remember! Let's break the images down into chunks.

Now we have **moon**, **star** and **moon**, **moon**. That is only two items to remember.

1. Look at the images below. Repeat their names three times.

2. Now close your eyes and say their names aloud.

65

Chunking

① Can you chunk these numbers together?
Write them in the space below by following the example.

4 5   _ _

② Close your eyes and say the numbers aloud.

③ Can you chunk the shapes below together?
Write their names or draw them in the space.

circle   circle   heart   triangle   circle

④ Close your eyes and say the shape names aloud.

You may need to repeat the chunking several times for you to remember it.

5. Can you chunk the insects below together? Write or draw them in the space.

6. Close your eyes and say the insect names aloud.

7. Can you chunk the objects below together? Write their names or draw them in the space.

8. Close your eyes and say the object names aloud.

Picture it!

Mind tool

The next tool is **visualization**. This is when we picture the information we are trying to remember in our heads.

1

star   triangle   star   circle

 Look at the shapes above. Take a mental picture.

a. Now close your eyes. Can you picture the shapes?
b. Next say the shape names aloud.
c. Open your eyes and check if you got them right.

2

fish   frog   frog   duck

a. Look at the animals above. Take a mental picture.
b. Now close your eyes. Can you picture the animals?
c. Next say the names of the animals aloud.
d. Open your eyes and check if you got them right.

You could ask a grown-up to check your answers.

Picture this

1

| apple | apple | banana | banana | lime |

a. Look at the fruits. Take a mental picture.
b. Now close your eyes. Can you picture the fruits?
c. Next say the names of the fruits aloud.
d. Open your eyes and check if you got them right.

2

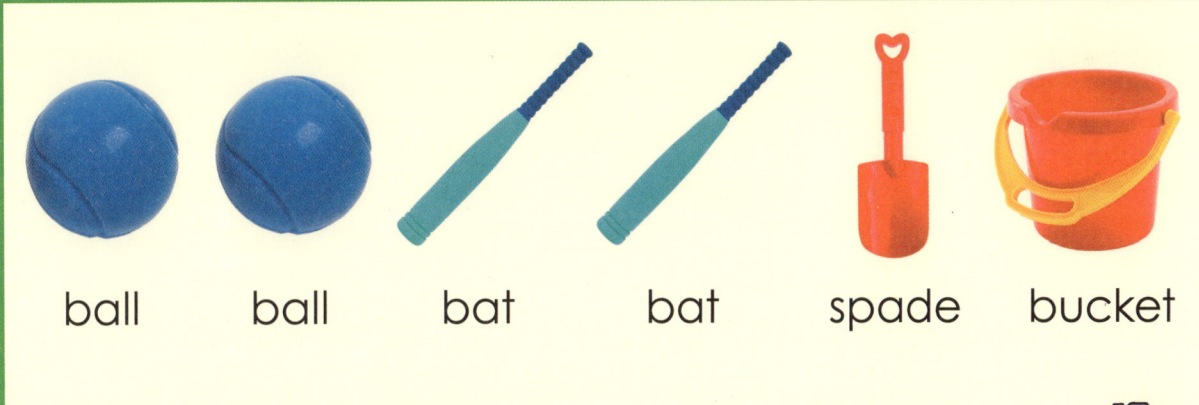

| ball | ball | bat | bat | spade | bucket |

a. Look at the objects. Take a mental picture.
b. Now close your eyes. Can you picture the objects?
c. Next say the names of the objects aloud.
d. Open your eyes and check if you got them right.

Letter sequences

Now we are going to practice remembering sequences of letters.

You will need your pull-out alphabet arc.

1. Let's try it together.
   Which tool will you use to remember the sequence?

2. Cover up the letters and write them in the space below.

3. Look at the letters below.
   Which tool will you use to remember this sequence?

4. Cover up the letters and write them in the space below.

Try touching the letters in the alphabet sequence. This will help you to remember them.

More sequences

1. Look at the letters below. Choose which tool you are going to use to remember the sequence.

2. Once you are ready, cover up the sequence above. Look for the letters in the box. Circle them.

m	s	r	e	q	v	f	o	y	i	z	l	k
b	p	g	d	w	c	n	a	h	t	x	u	j

Remember, use your bookmark!

3. Now uncover the sequence. Did you find all the letters?

4. Look at the letters below. Choose which tool you are going to use to remember the sequence.

Once you are ready, turn over the page.

Seeing letters in different fonts and sizes makes it easier for us to recognize them.

5. Making sure not to check back to page 71, look for the letters in the box below. Circle them.

m	s	r	h	q	v	g	o	y	i	z	l	k
b	p	f	d	w	c	n	a	e	t	x	u	j

6. Now check page 71. Did you find all the letters?

7. Look at the letters below.

8. Once you are ready, cover up the sequence above. Look for the letters in the box below. Circle them.

m	s	r	h	q	v	g	o	y	i	z	l	k
b	p	f	d	w	c	n	a	e	t	x	u	j

9. Now uncover the sequence. Did you find all the letters?

Try a different memory tool if you find it hard to remember the sequence.

Picture memory

1 Look at these pictures for two minutes. Try to remember as many things as you can.

Which memory tool will you use?

2 Now cover them up. How many things can you remember? Write or draw them in the boxes below, or you could ask a grown-up to help.

1	2	3
4	5	6

Uncover the pictures. Did you find them all? If not, you could try again!

Remember it!

   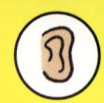

1 Look at these pictures for two minutes. Try to remember as many things as you can.

2 Now cover them up. How many things can you remember? Write or draw them in the boxes below, or you could ask a grown-up to help.

1	2	3
4	5	6

Now check the pictures above to see how many you got right.

Copy me

1. Can you copy the sequence by repeating the actions?

stretch   star jump   hop   touch your toes

Which tool will you use to remember the sequence? Chunking, repetition, or visualization?

2. Can you copy the sequence by repeating the actions?

sit   star jump   star jump   touch your toes

Try out a different tool for each sequence. Which worked best?

Memory dots

1. Can you visualize the dot-to-dot pattern on the left-hand side of the grid? Remember to take a mental picture.

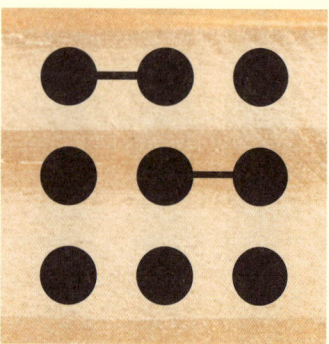
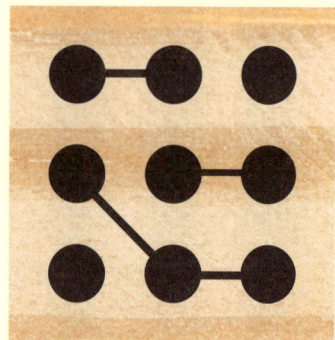
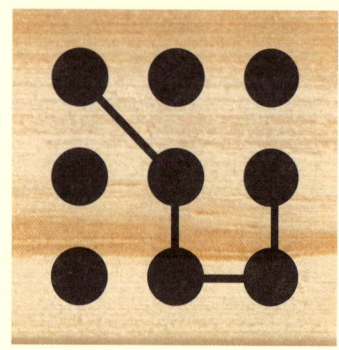

2. Cover up the pattern on the left side. Draw in the pattern on the right side.

3. How many patterns did you get right?

Remember, use your bookmark!

My house

1. Ask a grown-up to read each of the instructions below.

   - Color the front door red
   - Color the windows blue
   - Color the chimney green
   - Color the roof yellow
   - Color the fence orange
   - Color the walls purple

2. Cover up Activity 1. Using a memory tool, color in the house by following the instructions.

Remember, use your bookmark!

Did you choose repetition, chunking, or visualization?

77

Bouncy balls

1. Can you remember the pattern of these balls?

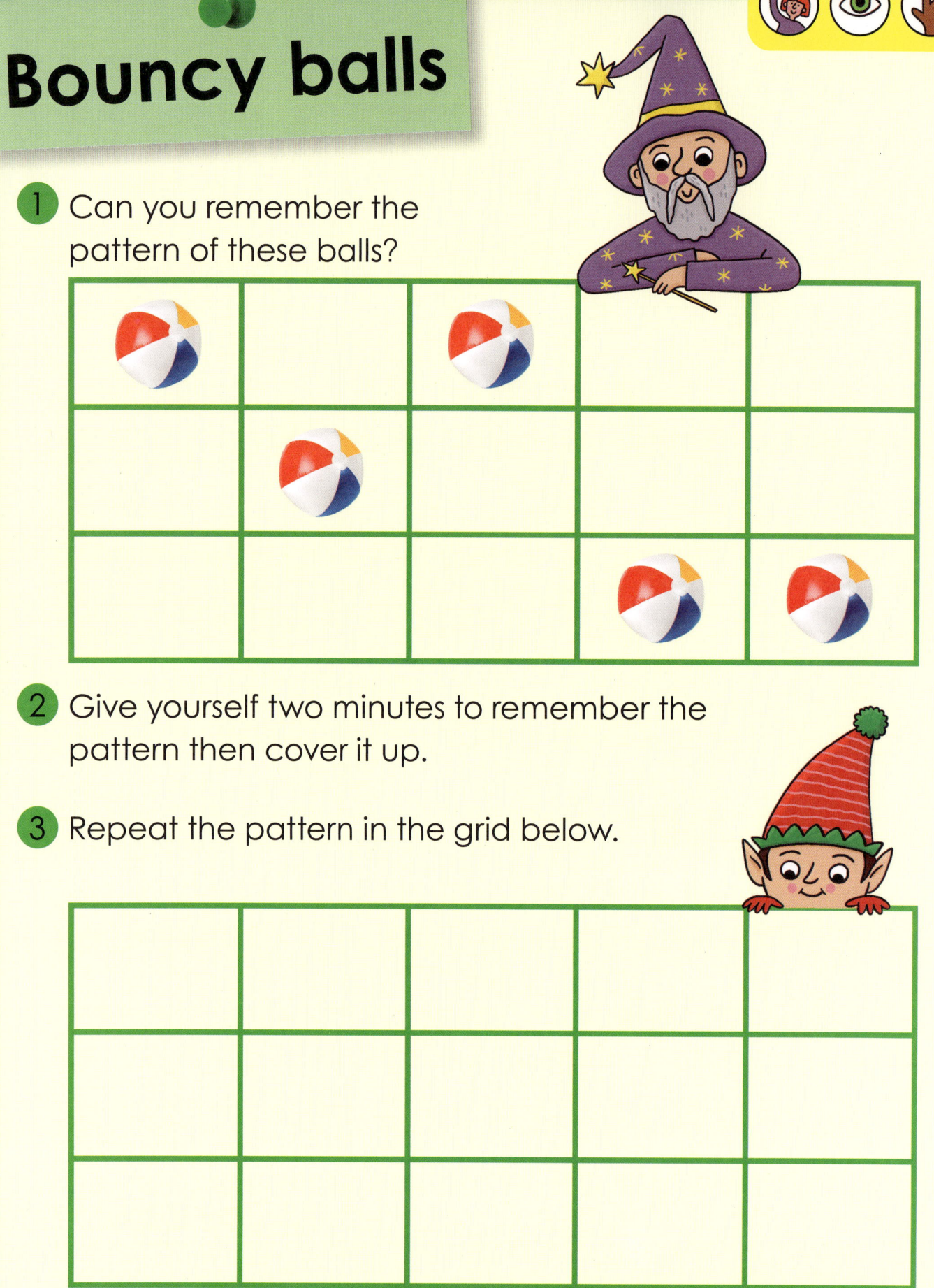

2. Give yourself two minutes to remember the pattern then cover it up.

3. Repeat the pattern in the grid below.

Dino world

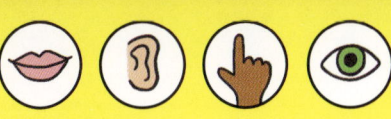

1. Look at the dinosaur scene below. Try to remember the image.

You could:
- repeat what you can see
- chunk different parts of the picture together
- visualize the picture

2. Now turn over the page.

It may help to do this activity in a quiet place.

③ Now look at the dinosaur scene below.

④ Can you find the five differences between the two pictures? Color in a footprint for each difference you find.

If you didn't find all the differences, go back and try again. You could try a different memory tool.

Which sentence?

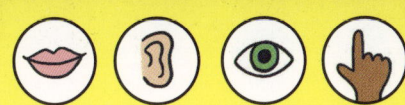

1. Read the two sentences.

The dog went on a walk.

The cat played outside.

2. Cover up the sentences and pictures.
   Which sentence came first? Write it out below.

_____

Remember, use your bookmark!

3. Read the two sentences.

He likes to paint.

She likes to run.

4. Cover up the sentences and pictures.
   Which sentence came second? Write it out below.

_____

Listen and color

1. Ask a grown-up to read these instructions to you.

   - Color the parrot's wings red
   - Color the parrot's beak blue
   - Color the parrot's feet purple
   - Color the parrot's body yellow
   - Color the parrot's eye orange

2. Cover up Activity 1. Using a memory tool, color in the parrot by following the instructions.

Listen and color

1 Ask a grown-up to read these instructions to you.

- Color the tractor's wheels black
- Color the tractor's lights yellow
- Color the tractor's chimney red
- Color the tractor's cab green
- Color the pig pink

2 Cover up Activity 1. Using a memory tool, color in the tractor by following the instructions.

Copy image

1. Look at the pictures in the grid below.

2. Now cover up the pictures.

Say the pictures aloud so that you are using two senses. This will make it easier to remember.

84

3 Can you remember all the pictures from Activity 1? Draw them in the correct place in the grid below.

Choose a memory tool to help you remember the pictures.

4 How many pictures did you get right?

Tricky words

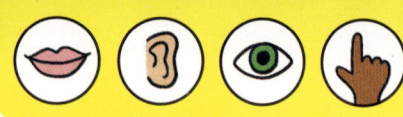

Help your child to remember tricky words using the memory tools they have learned.

Let's practice with the word "some."
This is a sequence of 4 letters.

Are you going to repeat three times? "some" "some" "some"
Are you going to chunk? "so" "me"
Are you going to take a mental picture and visualize?

1 Can you spell these words using your memory tools?

push

 Cover the word.

 Now spell it: _____

Check. Did you get it right? ☐

Remember, use your bookmark!

put

 Cover the word.

 Now spell it: _____

 Check. Did you get it right?

86

said

Cover the word.

Now spell it: _____

Check. Did you get it right? ☐

says

Cover the word.

Now spell it: _____

Check. Did you get it right? ☐

school

Cover the word.

Now spell it: _____

Check. Did you get it right? ☐

does

Cover the word.

Now spell it: _____

Check. Did you get it right? ☐

Sight words

Here is a list of common sight words.

1 Can you use the memory tools to learn them all?

all	he	there
am	into	they
are	must	this
ate	no	too
be	our	under
black	out	want
brown	please	was
came	ran	well
did	ride	went
do	saw	what
eat	say	white
four	she	who
get	so	will
good	soon	with
have	that	yes

You could ask a grown-up to write out the words on flash cards.

READING

Parent tips: Reading

What is it?

Reading is not a skill that just happens naturally. **Reading needs to be taught and developed**. It requires instruction, guidance, and regular practice.

Some children, including those with dyslexia, will struggle to acquire these skills and will need to be taught tools to help them to become fluent and accurate readers.

Aim

Learning to read is more than just recognizing a word. Children also need to know about the topic they are reading about. They need to be able to **predict, infer, summarize,** and then **understand** the text they are reading.

CVC words

Another important step of reading development is to **practice decoding (reading)** and then **encoding (spelling)**.

Learning to read **CVC (consonant-vowel-consonant)** words is part of this. Children can first learn to read the individual sounds of the letters, then blend those sounds together to produce a whole word.

For example, the CVC word "cat" can be broken down into /c/ /a/ /t/. Children will say each sound in turn. Once they hear the sounds, they will be able to **blend** them back together to read the word "cat."

Once your child is confident with reading CVC words, they can progress to reading **CCVC (consonant-consonant-vowel-consonant)** words such as "swim" and **CVCC (consonant-vowel-consonant- consonant)** words such as "left."

Skills

The activities are designed to help your child practice these **skills**:

- **Decoding:** breaking down words into individual sounds.
- **Predict:** suggest what will happen in the future based on evidence from the text.
- **Infer:** conclusions they make based on evidence in the text.
- **Summarize:** identify the key points from the text.
- **Comprehend:** understand what they have read.

Tips

- Your child may need **adult help** for some of the activities in this section. These activities will have a special symbol by them.

- When **reading**, we refer to each letter by its sound rather than its letter name.

- We use / / symbols to represent a sound. Use the **letter chart** on the back cover to remind your child how to say the sounds.

Resources

Phonetically decodable books:
https://www.thereadingleague.org/decodable-text-sources/

91

High-frequency words

What is it?

- **High-frequency words** (or sight words) are words that appear most often in the English language.

- It is recommended that children can recognize these words by **sight**. This helps children to become better readers, as they won't need to break down unfamiliar words into individual sounds, before blending them back together to read the word.

- Many high-frequency words are also **common exception words**. Common exception words are words where the usual spelling rules do not apply. Examples of these words are: "climb," "door," and "Mr."

- There are **flash cards** of the first 20 words that children need to know by sight.

High-frequency words flash cards

- There are flash cards for **20 high-frequency words**.
- Carefully **press out** the flash cards to remove them from the book.
- Practice using the flash cards **daily** for no more than 10 minutes at a time. If this isn't possible, practice twice a week.

his

and

Tips

- Start with a small number of flash cards (around four). Once your child knows those cards by **sight**, add in another card, and then gradually increase.

said	it	she	but
to	of	on	his
a	I	they	at
and	he	you	for
the	in	was	is

can	what	went	not
we	her	have	some
all	my	this	like
with	had	out	be
that	are	there	up

High-frequency word search

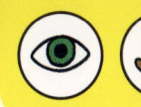

High-frequency words (sight words) are words that appear most often in the English language.

1. How many high-frequency words can you find in the word search? Following the example, circle each word and check the boxes.

- ☐ the
- ☐ and
- ☐ we
- ☐ to
- ☐ said
- ☐ in
- ☐ he
- ☐ can
- ☐ of
- ☐ it
- ✓ was
- ☐ you
- ☐ they
- ☐ on
- ☐ she
- ☐ is
- ☐ for
- ☐ at
- ☐ his
- ☐ but

f	a	s	r	y	o	u	l	h	e	q	p	c
y	t	h	e	j	d	s	a	i	u	n	c	a
r	h	v	b	x	a	t	m	s	q	e	o	n
r	t	f	o	r	y	g	a	n	d	j	u	k
s	l	m	f	h	b	f	v	d	s	t	c	x
a	z	i	u	w	p	i	t	g	d	o	e	i
i	q	n	v	e	b	h	j	(w	a	s)	k	s
d	f	k	g	t	z	s	h	e	v	j	f	b
h	b	u	t	x	n	p	g	q	t	h	e	y

Create your own

① Can you make your own word search using the following high-frequency words?

- ☐ up
- ☐ had
- ☐ my
- ☐ her
- ✓ what
- ☐ there
- ☐ out
- ☐ this
- ☐ have
- ☐ went
- ☐ be
- ☐ like

Add the high-frequency words in first by adding one letter into each box. After that, you can add in other letters to fill the grid.

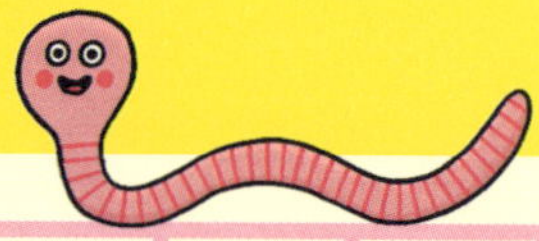

				w	h	a	t				

② Ask a friend to complete the word search. Did they find all the words?

Reading CVC words

CVC words are words that are "consonant-vowel-consonant," for example: /p/ /i/ /g/.

1 Can you read the CVC words?

top — van — hat — jam — fox — log — mop — cup — pin — tip — dog — mug — pet — beg — sip — vet — tub — set — cat — pig — net — web — ten

Remember, you can break the word down into individual sounds and blend them together if you find the word difficult to read. For example, "jam" will be /j/ /a/ /m/.

Reading CCVC words

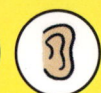

CCVC words are words that are "consonant-consonant-vowel-consonant." They include consonant blends (two letters producing one sound), for example, /f/ /r/ /o/ /g/.

1 Can you read the CCVC words?

grab, trap, flag, plot, grid, sled, slab, step, grin, chin, spit, clog, clap, glad, slug, crop, bled, skid

If you are unsure, remember to break the word down into individual sounds, then blend them back together. For example, "grab" is /g/ /r/ /a/ /b/.

Reading CVCC words

CVCC words are words that are "consonant-vowel-consonant-consonant," for example, /s/ /i/ /n/ /g/.

1 Can you read the CVCC words?

band
raft
sift
pond
lost
wild

rang
bump
help
lump
dunk
long

belt
send
pant
milk
salt
sand

If you are unsure, remember to break the word down into individual sounds and then blend them together. For example, "milk" is /m/ /i/ /l/ /k/.

Four in a row

1 Can you find four words in a row that have the same vowel sounds? There is a set to find for each of the five vowels. Color each set of vowels a different color.

cat	map	sing	salt	wild
raft	flat	fling	rag	sift
peg	dog	flag	trap	lip
leg	log	milk	tap	swim
jet	box	sang	fat	lump
grand	tot	felt	sent	pant
bend	cup	but	mug	dunk

Remember, the five vowel sounds are a, e, i, o, and u.

100

Complete the sentence

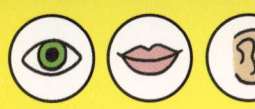

1 Can you complete the sentences by writing in the missing words?

| fly | Max | smell | some | pet |

The bird can _ _ _ .

_ _ _ runs fast.

You can _ _ _ _ _ with your nose.

Jim has a _ _ _ .

I would like _ _ _ _ candy.

More sentences

1 Can you complete the sentences by writing in the missing words?

| tidy | bake | game | fan | late |

I will _ _ _ _ up my pens.

Alex wants to _ _ _ _ a cake.

I was _ _ _ _ for school.

Can we play a _ _ _ _ ?

Turn on the _ _ _ .

Understand the text

Help your child to take information from the text so they can understand what it is about.

1. Ask a grown-up to read this passage with you.

> **Dogs**
> It is thought that dogs are the most popular pet in the world. They are called this because they are known for being friendly, loyal, and caring. There are over 300 different breeds of dogs in the world. The most popular type of dog is called a Labrador.

Now answer the following questions.

2. How many different breeds of dog are there in the world? Circle your answer.

   a. 300
   b. 250
   c. 500
   d. 100

3. What are dogs known for?

   _____

4. What is the most popular type of dog?

   _____

Remember, you can read the text again to find the answers.

My alien

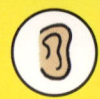

1 Follow the instructions to color in the picture of the alien's face.

- My alien's hair is yellow
- My alien's eyes are red
- My alien's lips are green
- My alien's face is blue
- My alien's ears are pink
- My alien's nose is orange

Summarizing

Summarizing means to take the most important parts of the text and put them into your own words.

1 Ask a grown-up to read this passage with you.

> **School**
> In the United Kingdom, children start school at the age of four or five years old. In other countries, such as China, children start school at six years old. Most classes have around 30 children in them, but in China, most classes have around 50 children.

2 Can you write down three main points from the text?

1. _____

2. _____

3. _____

Remember, you shouldn't change what the text means, add new things, or take away important information.

Time for school

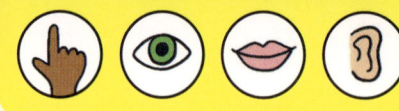

Inference means taking a guess about something you don't know for sure, based on the information available in the text.

1 The children are going to school.

2 Can you spot three things in the picture that tell you the children are going to school?

1. _____

2. _____

3. _____

Can you see any of the things you need for school in the picture? Do those things tell us anything about the children?

Beach day

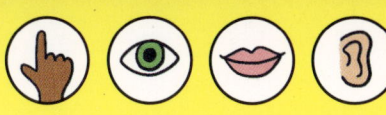

1 The children are going to the beach.

2 Can you spot three things in the picture that tell you the children are going to the beach?

1. _____

2. _____

3. _____

Happy birthday!

  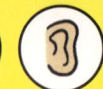

1 It is Sam's birthday. He is 8 years old.

2 Can you spot three things in the picture that tell you that Sam is 8 years old?

1. _____

2. _____

3. _____

WRITING

Parent tips: Writing

What is it?

Children with dyslexia often find **writing** challenging. There can be many reasons for this:

- Your child may have **good ideas** but struggle to transfer these ideas onto paper.

- Your child may find writing challenging, as they are constantly having to stop to consider how to **spell** a word.

- Your child may not like making mistakes in their writing. They could spend a lot of **time** trying to think of replacement words that they can spell rather than completing their work. This means they are unable to finish their writing in the time given.

- Your child may struggle to organize and **structure** their writing.

Handwriting style

Earlier in the book, we practiced a **manuscript handwriting style** on the handwriting sheets on pages 33 and 34. You should continue to practice this handwriting style or the handwriting style used by your child's school in this section.

Developing a handwriting style will help to build the **automatic recall** of which strings of letters belong together. This will also help spelling to become more automatic.

Holding a pencil

There is a **tip sheet** on the inside front cover that advises how to help children hold a pencil correctly.

Skills

- **Handwriting** practice to help develop an understanding of how different letters join

- Preplanning **strategies** to assist with transferring ideas onto paper

- Expanding **simple sentences** to add description or a clause

- Developing an understanding of **grammar**

Tips

- Each school has its **own policy** on handwriting, and you should consult this policy to support your child at home.

- Your child can practice individual letters in a manuscript handwriting style using the **practice sheets** on pages 33 and 34.

- It is recommended that **handwriting** is practiced regularly so it becomes an automatic skill.

Spider diagram

A spider diagram is a useful tool to help plan ideas when writing.

1 Look at the picture in the middle of the spider diagram.

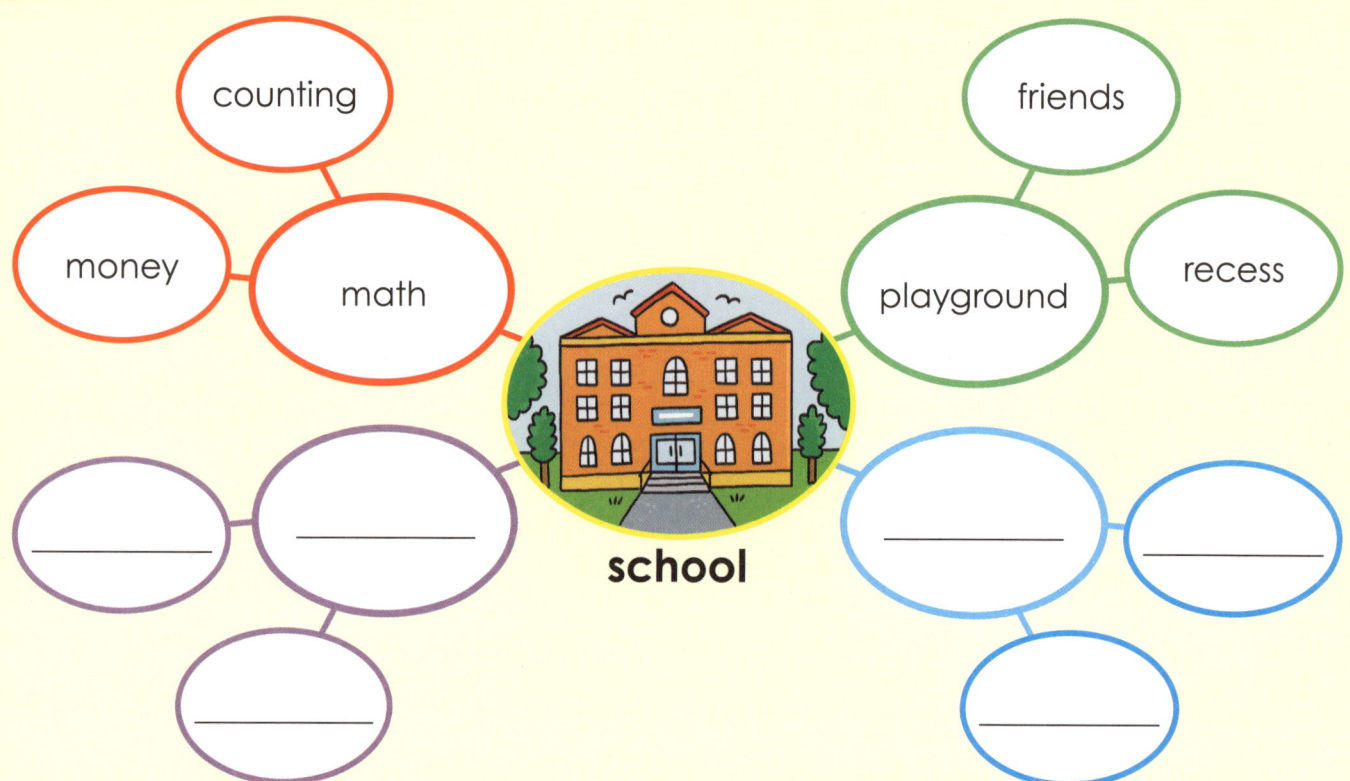

school

2 There are four main branches on the outside of the spider diagram. Can you think of two other ideas or objects that might relate to the picture?

Add these to your spider diagram on the next page.

3 Now that you have completed the four main branches, look at each branch in turn. There are two smaller branches coming off each main branch. These are for you to add extra ideas about a topic.

Add these to your spider diagram on the next page.

My spider diagram

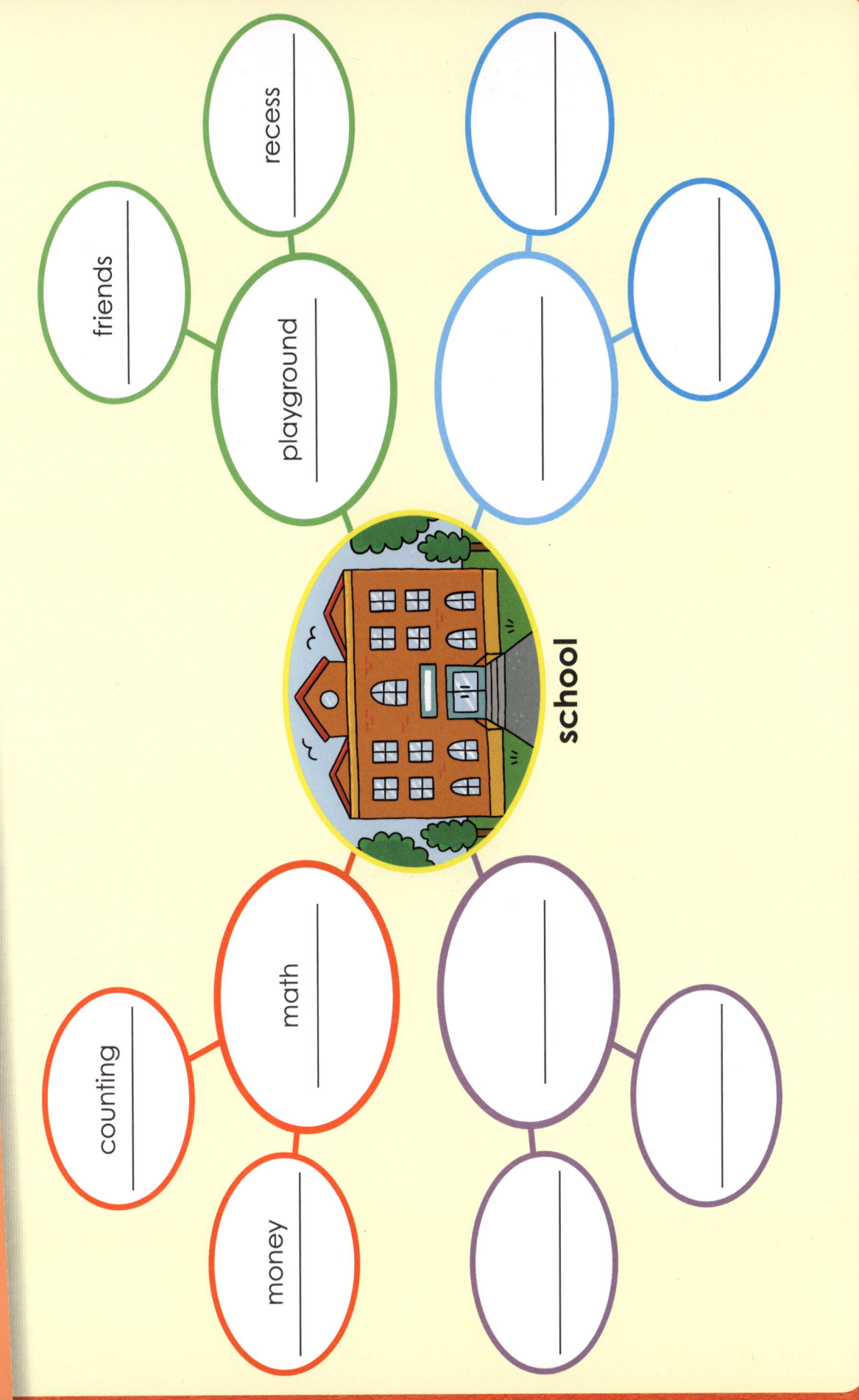

Writing sentences

Choose one of the branches from the spider diagram on the previous page.

1 Can you turn each of those key words into sentences? For example, the key word here is **recess**:

> My favorite time of day is **recess**.

> At **recess** I get to see my friends.

> We usually play tag on the playground at **recess**, which is fun!

2 Now you try! Write sentences about five key words below.

1. _____

2. _____

3. _____

4. _____

5. _____

Build on a sentence

Expanding sentences is a way to add more detail to make a sentence more interesting or to provide extra information.

1. Can you write a sentence of your own based on one of the pictures below?

| dog | store | park |

For example: The dog went on a walk.

Your turn: _____

_____

_____

_____

115

2 Now can you add one of the conjunctions to your sentence?

| for | and | nor | but | or | yet | so |

Conjunction words are used to connect words or phrases together.

For example: The dog went on a walk, but it started to rain.

Your turn: _____

_____

3 Can you now add a describing word? Here are some examples:

| small | brown | big | busy | tall |
| green | happy | short | angry | funny |

Did you know that describing words are also called adjectives?

For example: The brown dog went on a walk, but it started to rain.

Your turn: _____

_____

Read your sentence aloud. Does it make sense?

116

Choose again

1 Choose one of the pictures below and write another simple sentence:

| beach | cat | bedroom |

Your turn: _____
_____

2 Now add a conjunction:

| for | and | nor | but | or | yet | so |

Your turn: _____
_____

3 Now add a describing word:

Your turn: _____
_____

Refer back to page 116 if you aren't sure of a describing word to use.

Free-write

1. Choose a topic that you want to write about. Write this in the middle of your spider diagram on page 119.

   You could write about pets, music, sports, or anything you like.

2. Think of four things based on your topic that you would like to write about. Write these on the main branches of the spider diagram on page 119.

3. Choose two other ideas or objects to write about your topic. Add them to the smaller branches of the spider diagram on page 119.

4. Use your spider diagram from page 119 to write about your chosen topic. Remember to expand your sentences using conjunctions and describing words.

   Do not worry about spelling, punctuation, or grammar. These can be edited later.

Your topic: _____

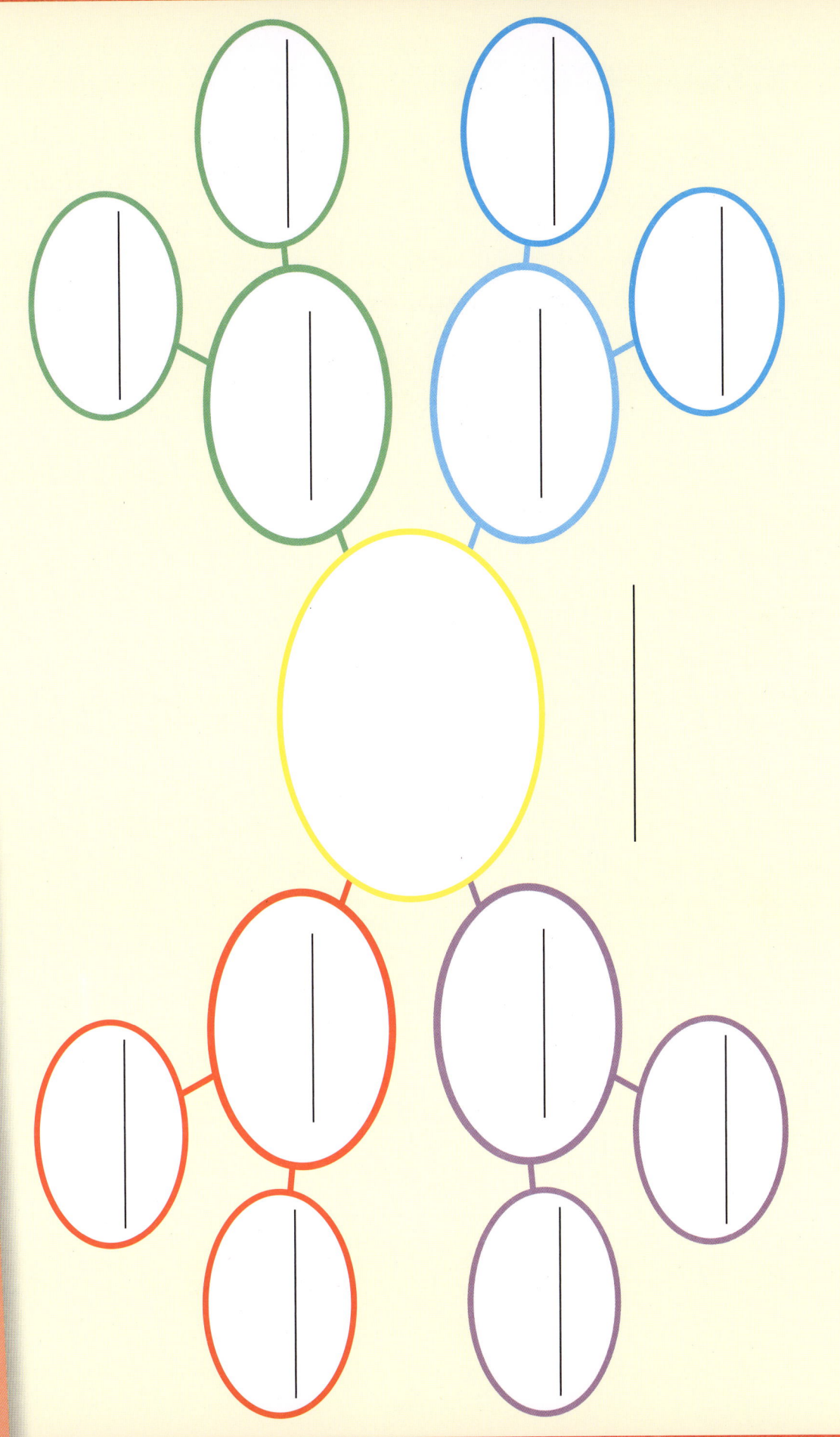

Create your own

Answers

Page 10
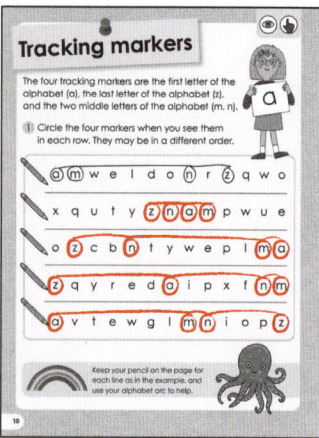

Page 11

Page 12
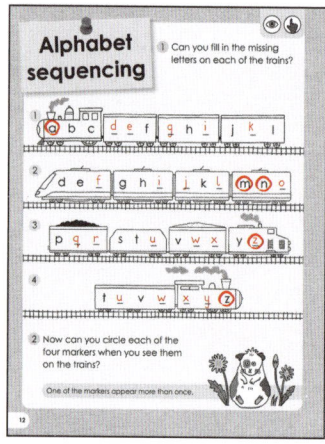

Page 14

Page 16
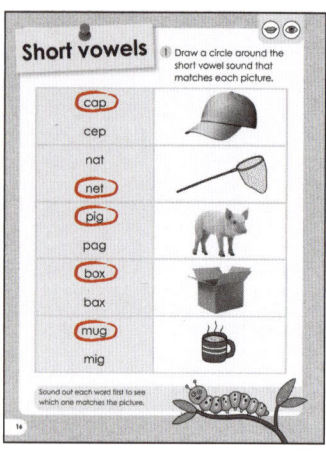

Page 17
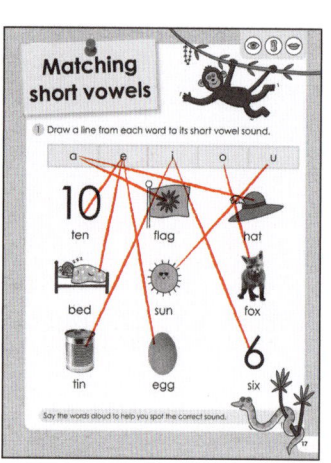

Page 18
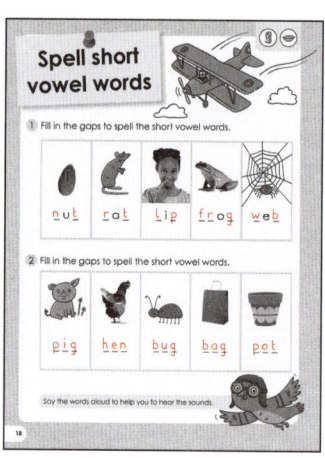

Page 19

Page 20

Page 21
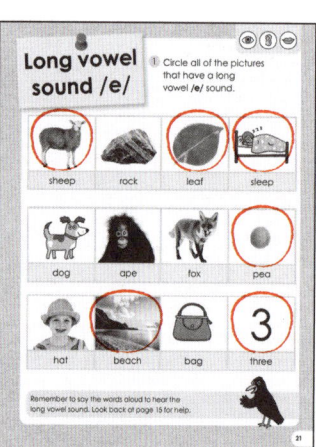

Page 22

Page 23
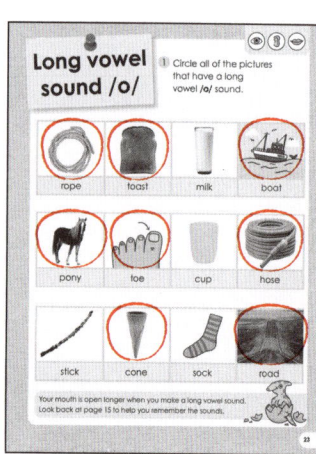

Page 24
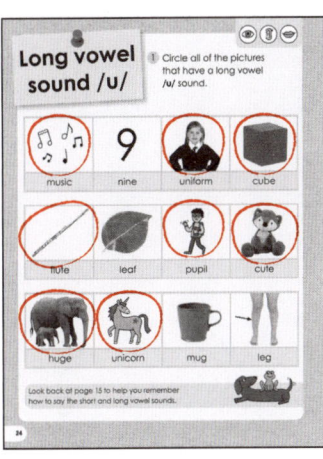

Page 25

Page 26
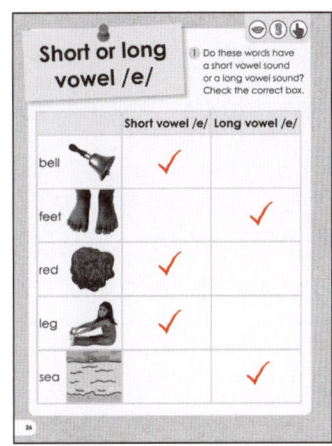

Page 27

Page 28
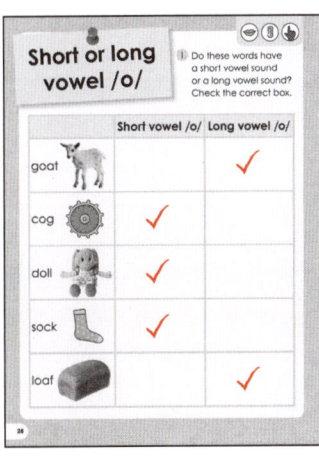

Page 29
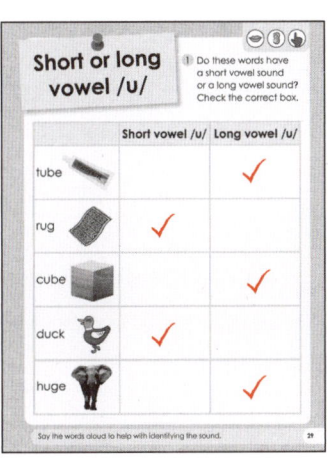

Page 30
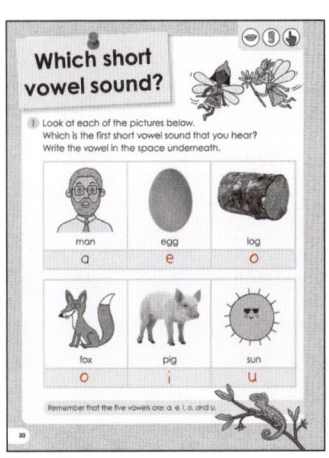

Page 31
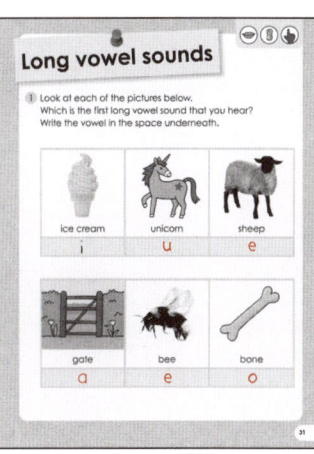

Page 32
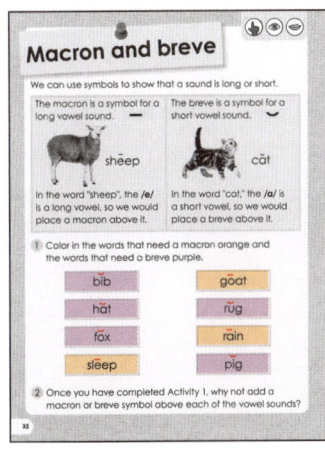

Page 38
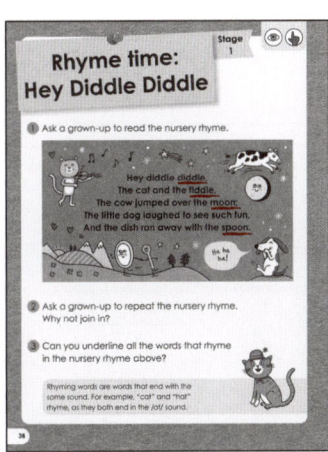

Page 39

Page 40

Answers

Page 41

Page 42

Page 43

Page 44

Page 45
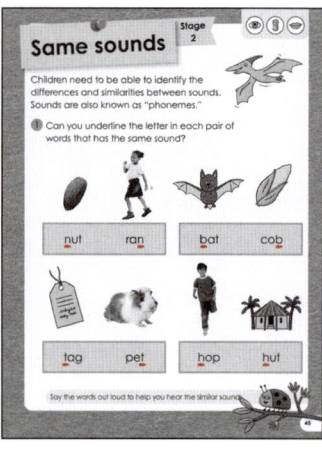

Page 46
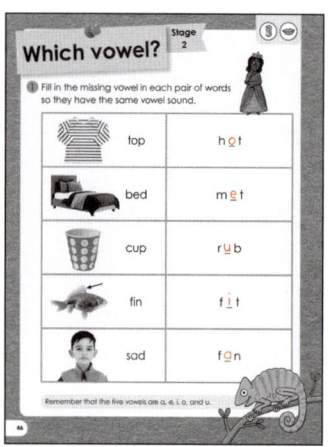

Page 47

Page 48

Page 49
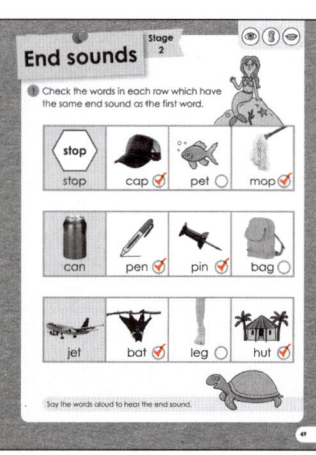

Page 50

Page 51

Page 52
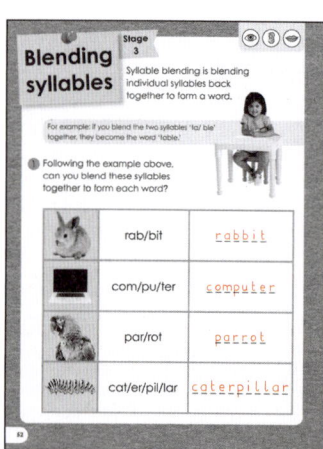

Page 53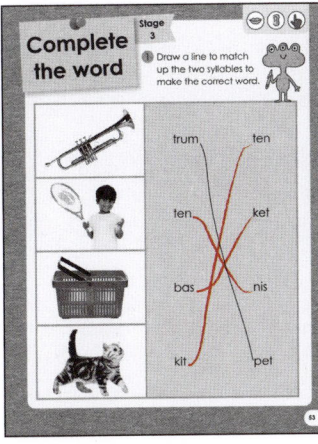

Page 54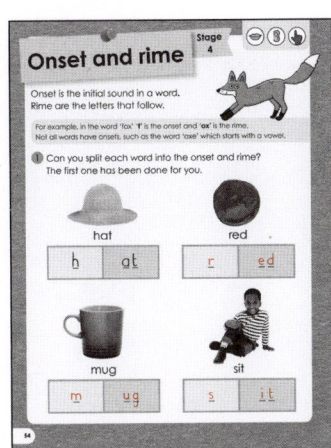

Page 55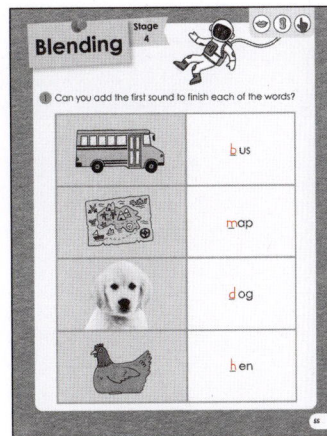

Page 56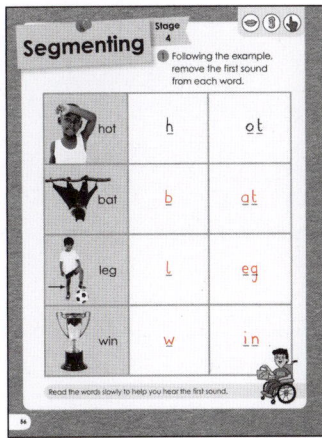

Page 57

Page 58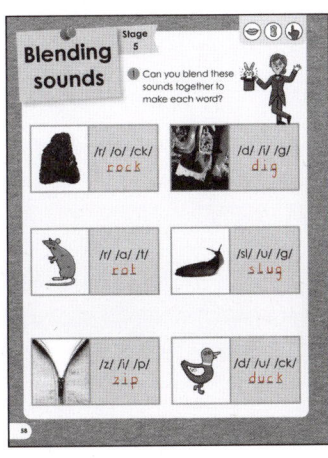

Page 63

Page 64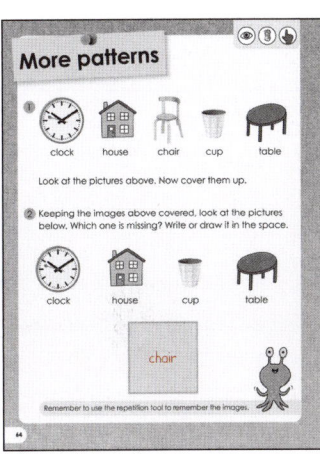

Page 66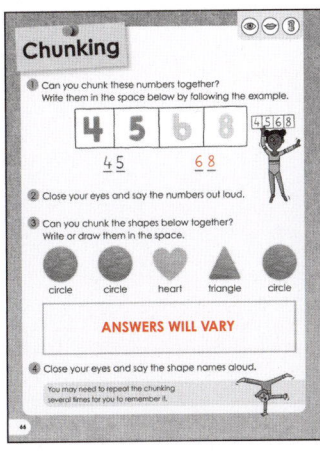

Page 70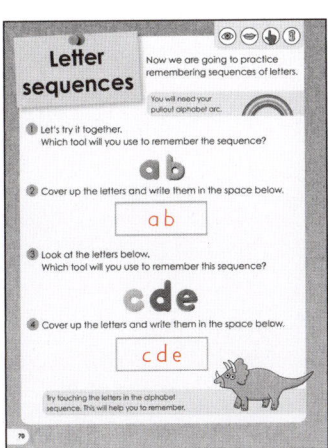

Page 71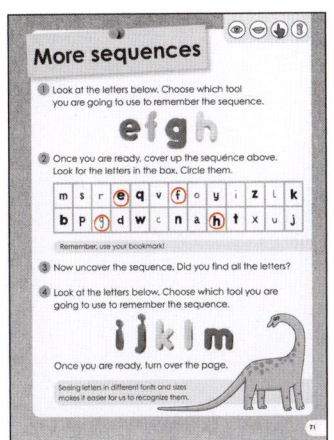

Page 72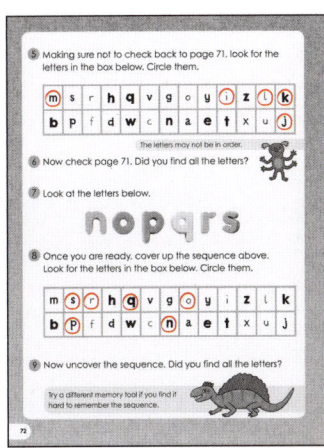

Answers

Page 76
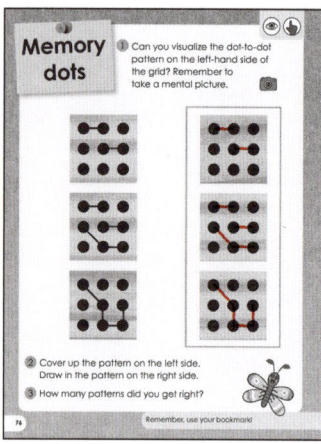

Page 77
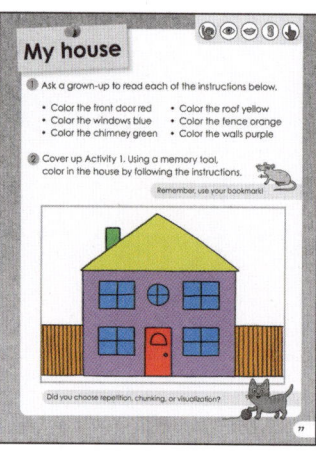

Page 78

Page 80

Page 81

Page 82

Page 83

Page 86

Page 87

Page 95
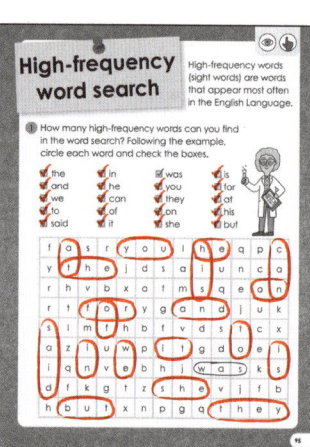

Page 100
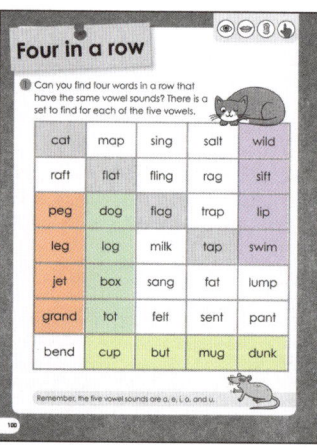

Page 101

Page 102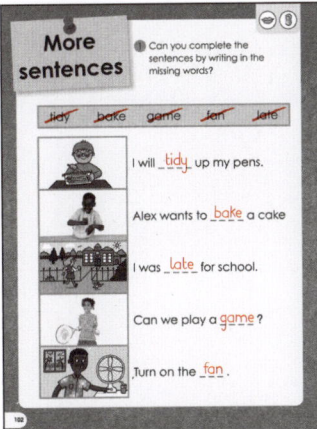

Page 103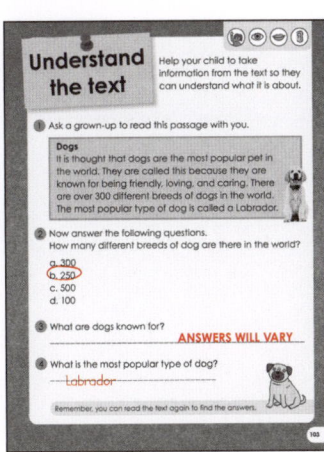

Page 104

Glossary

Automaticity: The ability to complete a task automatically and without much thought.

Common exception words: Words where the usual spelling rules do not apply.

Comprehend: The ability to understand the text that has been read or listened to, as well as the ability to retrieve, infer, and summarize information from text.

Dyslexia: A specific learning difficulty that causes difficulties with phonological awareness, verbal memory, and verbal processing speed. This has a negative impact on literacy skills like reading, writing, and spelling.

Dual coding: The method of using two (or more) stimuli to learn information, e.g., spelling a word by writing it down and saying the letter names at the same time.

Decoding (reading): When words are broken down into individual sounds, e.g., the word "cat" is broken down into the sounds /c/ /a/ /t/.

Encoding (spelling): When individual sounds are blended to produce a word, e.g., /d/ /o/ /g/ becomes "dog."

Fluency: The ability to smoothly articulate sounds while reading with accuracy and expression.

High-Frequency Words: High-Frequency Words are words that appear the most often in written text.

Infer: In comprehension, infer is to conclude from evidence in the text what has happened.

Letter-sound correspondence (matching letter sounds to names): The relationship between the letters in the alphabet and the sounds that they produce, e.g., knowing that the letter "s" can produce a /s/ sound as in "silly."

Macron and breve: A macron (¯) is a symbol used to represent a long vowel sound. A breve (˘) is a symbol used to represent a short vowel sound.

Multisensory teaching: The process of using multiple senses simultaneously to teach a new concept.

Onset and rime: The onset is the section of a word that comes before the vowel. The rime is the section of a word that starts with the vowel and includes all of the following letters. Not all words have an onset.

Phonemes: A unit of sound.

Phonemic awareness: The ability to identify individual sounds within words and manipulate them.

Phonics: Matching individual sounds to their corresponding letters / groups of letters.

Phonological awareness: The understanding of the sound structure of words.

Predict: In comprehension, prediction is using the text to guess what will happen next without reading the text.

Summarize: In comprehension, this is the ability to identify the most important points in a story and retell them to provide an overview of the text.

Syllabification: The process of breaking words into their individual syllables to read or spell a word accurately. A syllable is a unit of sound with one vowel sound.

Verbal memory: The ability to deal with and remember what we hear, such as following instructions.

Verbal processing speed: The time taken to process and respond to verbal information, such as language.

Visual memory: The ability to deal with and remember information presented in a visual format.

Working memory: Allows us to temporarily hold a small amount of information while completing tasks.

Additional resources

Current research on dyslexia:
https://dyslexia.yale.edu/

Fact sheets from the International Dyslexia Association (IDA):
https://dyslexiaida.org/fact-sheets/

Contact the Orton-Gillingham Academy for a list of tutors in your state:
https://www.ortonacademy.org/

Decodable text sources:
https://www.thereadingleague.org/decodable-text-sources/

Pronunciation of 44 phonemes (sounds):
https://youtu.be/wBuA589kfMg

Author biographies

Rebecca Heyes is a dyslexia and dyscalculia specialist and teacher. She has a passion for learning, and in addition to her teacher training degree, has completed further degrees in dyslexia, dyscalculia, and special educational needs. Rebecca has a wealth of experience and currently works with numerous schools, colleges, and universities across England, UK, to support both teaching staff in the form of training, and students in the form of assessments and tuition. In addition, Rebecca works as an associate tutor at a leading university in the field of dyslexia and dyscalculia.

Rebecca currently lives in the northwest of England, UK, with her two dogs, who love traveling with her around the country in her RV. She also owns two horses, a flock of hens, and three pygmy goats . . . and a cat who she describes as more work than all her other pets put together!

Kim Nau has an MS from Hofstra University, and she is a full-time dyslexia therapist. She is a certified member and fellow with the prestigious Orton-Gillingham Academy. She is also a certified structured literacy/dyslexia specialist from the Center for Effective Reading Instruction.

Kim has had a wide-ranging teaching career with experience working with a varied population of students. She began her teaching career in New York City 25 years ago as a classroom teacher in Brooklyn, New York, and then moved on to teaching English to speakers of other languages at local colleges.

Kim tutors remotely and lives in New York with her family and two Cavalier King Charles spaniels.

Contributors & credits

Educational Consultants: Rebecca Heyes & Kim Nau F/OGA
Senior Editor: Natalie Munday
Senior Designers: Rhea Gaughan & Sadie Thomas
Senior Production Controller: Ben Plagerson
Cover illustrations by Lee Cosgrove
Interior illustrations by Sophie Foster

Please note: Priddy Books does not have any control over, or responsibility for, any author or third-party websites or hyperlinks in or on this book.

Images credited to iStock Photo: Acorn & Ice cream cone © subjug; Fan © sunstock; Pine tree © 26ISO; Igloo © WesAbrams; Kite © Elementallmaging; Gem © Byjeng; Van © deepblue4you; Zebra © prapassong; Rainbow © Dragovich148; Pizza © Valengilda; Medal © RichVintage; Grape © masa44; Cap © akinshin; Frog, Chimpanzee, Fox Cub, Chicken, Sheep, Fox, Pony, Kid, & Cow © GlobalP; Piglet © Tsekhmister; Ice cream © stockphoto24; Oatmeal © Avalon_Studio; Cardboard box © Liudmila Chernetska; Can © Eivaisla; Nut © pidjoe; Flower pot © Anna Terekhova; Paper bag © s-cphoto; Log © bong hyunjung; Lake © SeanXu; Beach © Adam-Springer; Spices © Natalia Lipatova; Rice © bonchan; Beans © Pannonia; Train © scanrail; Chicken © suriyasilsaksom; Hose © futureimage; Stick © ivanastar; Cake © yumehana; Cat © bahadir-yeniceri; Baby © lostinbids; Toothpaste © skodonnell; Elephant © johan63; Ice cream © viennetta; Bee © antagain; Kitten © LightFieldStudios; Carrot © kolesnikovserg; Guinea pig © ?hsan Ero?lu; Green cap © s-cphoto; Girl © max-kegfire; Pot © sanddebeautheil; Black pin © MicroStockHub; Bed © Artem Perevozchikov; Mat © Feverpitched; Mime artist © Victoria Gnatiuk; Green tick © Bogdan Populov; Cap © taviox; Mop © indigolotos; Can © karandaev; Jet © marcokopp; Tiger © luamduan; Dinosaur © warpaintcobra; Helicopter © andsem; Computer © cinoby; Parrot © antagain; Caterpillar © prettyzhizhi; Straw hat © LoraLiu; Puppy © DieterMeyrl; Trophy © Valerie Loiseleux; Fog © WLDavies; Rock © miriam-doerr; Dig © cjp; Slug © ajt; Zip © fotyma; Fish © marrio31; Cupcake © RuthBlack; Sweet © Maxim Goulidow; Moon © Onfokus; Star © Smileus; Numbers © sxpnz; Butterfly © proxyminder; Spider © Andreas Häuslbetz; Orange flower & purple flower © VIDOK; Duck © Mac99; Fridge letters © kemie; Kitten © Viorika; Girl jumping © monkeybusinessimages; Wooden block © GooMmnutt; Kitten playing © stock_colors; Boy painting © Zinkevych; Car © Vladimiroquai; Tree © DNY59; Tart © boblin; Dog © feedough; Seabird © Gerald Corsi; Man & dog © 4x6; Running dog © Fly View Productions; City park © DS70; Beach © CAP53; Cat in garden © REMAINS; Boy in bedroom © DGLimages.

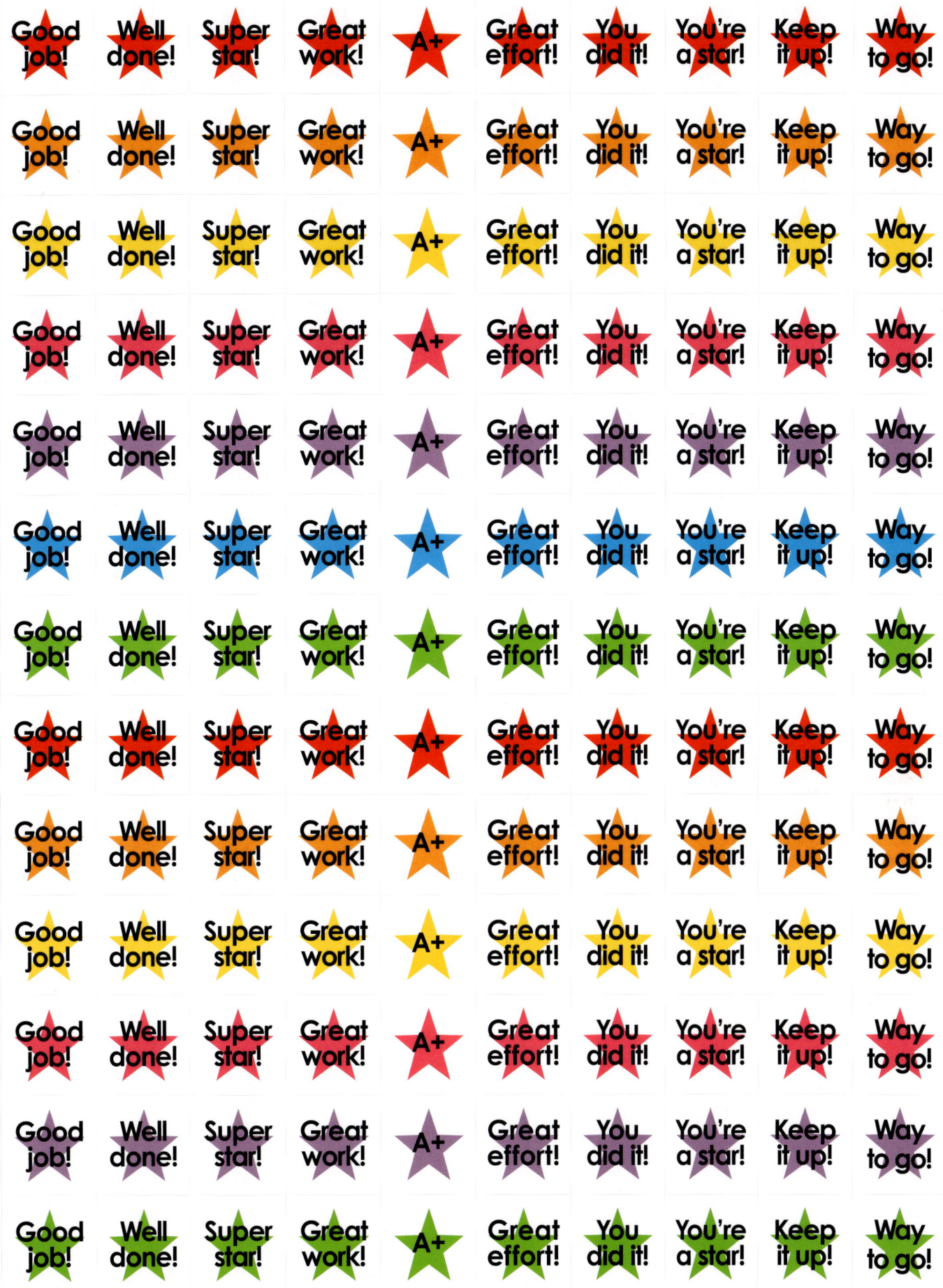